David Fulton Publishers Ltd
2 Barbon Close, London WC1N 3JX

First published in Great Britain by
David Fulton Publishers 1996

Note: The right of Jean Rudduck, Roland Chaplain and Gwen Wallace to be identified as the editors of this work has been asserted by them in accordance with the Copyright, Designs and Patents Act 1988.

British Library Cataloguing in Publication Data

A catalogue record for this book is available from the British Library

ISBN 1-85346-393-0

Typeset by Textype Typesetters, Cambridge
Printed in Great Britain by BPC Books and Journals Ltd., Exeter

Contents

Introduction

CHAPTER 1

Pupil voices and school improvement

Jean Rudduck, Roland Chaplain and Gwen Wallace

If schooling is going to make sense to children, let alone appeal to them, we must assume certain responsibilities. First, we should carefully examine the experiences that students undergo. The examination of experiences which result from institutional aspects of school life is especially urgent because they have received superficial study up 'til now. Second, we must make a conscious decision to alter conditions that create undesirable experiences. Third, we must communicate clearly to students the goals and expectations we believe make sense. And, fourth, we should affirm the right of students to negotiate our purposes and demands so that the activities we undertake with them have greatest possible meaning to all.

(Silberman, 1971, p. 364)

Silberman's words, written over twenty years ago, provide the agenda for this book. While there have been, in the interim, many studies of pupils' experiences in secondary schools, there is no expectation that accounts of their experiences should be drawn on to guide the development of school improvement strategies – nor, indeed, that pupils[1] themselves should be consulted so that we can hear their views at first hand. Our argument in this book is that what pupils say about teaching, learning and schooling is not only worth listening to but provides an important – perhaps the most important – foundation for thinking about ways of improving schools. Our broad summary of what pupils have told us in interview is that while teachers are for the most part supportive, stimulating and selfless in the hours they put in to help young people, the *conditions of learning* that are common across secondary schools do not adequately take account of the social maturity of young people, nor of the tensions and pressures they feel as they struggle to reconcile the demands of their social and personal lives with the development of their identity as learners.

Sonia Nieto (1994) confirms our view of what matters. She writes:

> Educating students today is a far different and more complex proposition than it has been in the past…Reforming school structures alone will not lead to differences in student achievement…if such changes are not accompanied by profound changes in how we as educators think about our students…One way to begin the process of changing school policies is to listen to students' views about them; however, research that focuses on student voice is relatively recent and scarce. (pp. 395;396)

Nieto points out that pupils' perspectives are for the most part missing in discussions concerning strategies for confronting educational problems and she also says – significantly, given the title of our book – that 'the voices of students are rarely heard in the debates about school failure and success' (p. 396). This view is echoed by Suzanne Soo Hoo (1993, p. 392) who says: 'Traditionally, students have been overlooked as valuable resources in the restructuring of schools'. At the same time Nieto adds a cautionary note, explaining that a focus on students 'is not meant to suggest that their ideas should be the final and conclusive word in how schools need to change'; to accept their words as the sole guide in school improvement is 'to accept a romantic view of students that is just as partial and condescending as excluding them completely from the discussions' (p. 398). The point we are making is that pupils' accounts of experience should be heard and should be taken seriously in debates about learning in secondary schools. (For additional support for this view see Schostak and Logan, 1984, and Lang, 1985.)

Patricia Phelan and her colleagues argue that it is important to give more attention to students' views of things that affect their learning – not so much factors outside school but those in school that teachers and policy makers have some power to change (1992, p. 696). Their interviews with students during the first two years of high school convinced them that 'students have a great deal to say about school and classroom conditions that educators should hear: about how students feel about themselves as learners and members of the school community, and their perceptions of the school as an educational and social setting.' However, the structuring of opportunities for dialogue between teachers and students in schools often assumes that the focus will be behaviour and not learning. If teachers have a view of students as young people to be managed as 'adversaries', then it is unlikely that they can unravel the power relationship and convince students that they genuinely want to enter into dialogue with them about learning, to hear and take their views seriously, and to become, as Phelan and her colleagues put it, 'co-conspirators in creating optimal learning situations' (p. 704).

School improvement: do pupil perspectives have a place?

At the moment, in the UK, the dominant concern is with enhancing the performance of pupils in the 16+ examinations. The preoccupation of school improvement researchers is to find ways of translating the common features of 'school effectiveness' into strategies and processes that will help schools to improve. It is not entirely clear whether the goal is a commitment to perpetual improvement or whether there is such a thing as an absolute state of effectiveness that schools can reach. What is clear is that it will take more than confession or meditation to reach the nirvana (or, as the dictionary defines it, 'the attainment of perfect beatitude')!

Nieto, as we saw above, argued that in the US, students' voices are rarely heard in the debates about school success and failure. Does this statement hold for the school improvement movement in this country? To some extent it does. Lang (1985, p. 172) distinguished research in which pupil views were sought 'in relation to some wider question and were therefore only considered in so far as they related to this question', and research where 'pupil perspectives were essentially the subject of the research work'. We would make a similar distinction in relation to school improvement studies. Some take into account the *inferred* experience of pupils and represent it in the researcher's construction of the situation; others provide commentaries which are the direct and deliberate result of consulting pupils about their experiences and seek to bring their authentic voices into the discourse of strategic planning. Although the burgeoning literature on school improvement centres on pupils and their attainments, there is little to suggest that the analyses of situations have taken into account the critiques which pupils can offer. Nor is it prominently suggested that those bent on improvement in schools might usefully start by inviting pupils to talk about what makes learning difficult for them, about what diminishes their motivation and engagement, and what makes some give up and others settle for a 'minimum risk, minimum effort' position – even though they know that doing well matters.

Our own interviews with pupils in secondary schools echo the observation of Phelan et al. that most pupils 'from all achievement levels and socio-cultural backgrounds want to succeed and want to be in an environment in which it is possible to do so' (1992, p. 696; see also 1994, p. 429). Behind the public mask of nonchalance that some pupils wear to hide their anxiety about the future is a concern to succeed and some realisation of the consequences of not making the grade. Some pupils (see chapter 12) arrive at this realisation too late to rebuild the foundation knowledge and skills that they will need to achieve in the 16+ assessment stakes. Their options are to stay in school and brave it out or to drop out; either alternative leads young people to seek out employment openings (often in their own extended families) where qualifications are not needed – a short-term strategy which runs counter to the government's proper concern to encourage young people to continue in education and training and to ensure that the country has a well-qualified work force.

Gray and Reynolds (in a chapter in *Merging Traditions: The Future of Research on School Effectiveness and School Improvement*) draw on Barber's work (1994) to summarise the main goals of 60 UK 'school improvement' projects. The most frequently cited targets were: lifting pupil attainment, raising expectations, and enhancing pupils' self-esteem and morale. In short, pupils are a key point of reference. The authors also refer to an earlier American study (Louis and Miles, 1992) which set out to discover what the impact was, three years on, of schools adopting so-called 'effective school' practices; 200 schools were included in the study. Many of the concerns were also pupil-oriented, as in the UK. The self-reports of the school principals suggested, somewhat confusingly, that it proved easier to change student attitudes to school (a positive shift was claimed by 49% of the sample) than to improve the student drop-out rate (where a positive shift was claimed by only 15% of the sample). What matters here is not so much what the headteachers and principals mean by their claims or whether their testimonies about the impact of their efforts in their own schools are to be fully believed, but that there is little indication – despite the central concern with pupils' well-being and attainment – as to whether the change strategies they adopted were based on any analysis of the situation that took account of pupils' perspectives. It seems illogical if the very people who are at the heart of these initiatives are not consulted about the things that might be done to help them to achieve. The point is carried home by the current preoccupation with bringing in new headteachers to turn around so-called 'failing' schools; we wonder whether, somewhere along the way, the crisis might have been averted if teachers had been able to work and plan constructively together, taking an agenda from pupils and using it as a basis for planned change.

A scrutiny of some of the various individual lists (and the aggregated summaries) of factors that, it is claimed, make a difference to school effectiveness leads us to make similar comments: pupils figure in these maps of concern as the ultimate beneficiaries but they do not feature among the people who might help to construct an analysis of the situation as a basis for determining strategy and helping to monitor its appropriateness. Let us look at some of these lists. The analysis offered by Gray et al. (1993) of ways in which a school might respond to patterns of underachievement identifies some useful short-term tactics – for example, changing the syllabuses, changing examination boards, entering more pupils for more examinations; targeting particular pupils at certain thresholds of attainment (such as those who have estimated grades of D in the 16+ examinations); building improved attainment targets into departmental development plans. It also identifies some longer-term tactics:

- challenging a 'closed door' mentality among staff;
- building cultures for discussing improvement issues at departmental and classroom levels;
- considering the extent to which school is already 'moving' and trying to reinforce an 'appetite' for change;
- fostering changes in approaches to leadership which encourage collaboration;
- providing better information about 'performance' across a number of areas;
- discussing changes to the ways in which teaching is undertaken.

Our response, predictably, would be to ask whether the discussion of improvement issues 'at the classroom level' assumes the involvement of pupils; whether approaches which encourage collaboration would include collaboration with pupils in monitoring and planning aspects of teaching and learning in the school; and whether discussion of the ways in which teaching is undertaken might involve pupils. Hopkins et al's list of conditions for school improvement (1994), while potentially radical (as Gray and Reynolds [in press] note), seems, nevertheless, to be almost entirely concerned with teachers:

- commitment to staff development;
- practical efforts to involve staff, students and community in school policies and decisions;
- transformational leadership;
- effective co-ordination strategies;
- attention to potential benefits of enquiry and reflection;
- commitment to collaborative planning.

There are no obvious spaces where pupil voices might be heard – except in the second item where the implications of bringing pupils in on 'school policies and decisions', depending on the scope and manner of their involvement, could well be profound. Beyond this, however, there is no apparent indication that the pupil voice may be important in shaping the agenda for improvement.

An analysis that is currently gaining ground (it was used, for instance, by the National Commission on Education in its recent study, *Success Against the Odds* [in press]) is that commissioned by OFSTED and constructed by Sammons, Hillman and Mortimore (1994). The list has a strong commonsense appeal. It suffers from the intrinsic weakness of all such lists – it lacks internal coherence and, as the authors acknowledge, there is no sense of the way in which the different items relate (nor perhaps could there be until the list is looked at in particular educational settings). Nevertheless, it remains a valuable resource for headteachers and their colleagues in drawing up an agenda for in-school monitoring and enquiry:

1. Professional identity	Firm and purposeful A participative approach The leading professional
2. Shared vision and goals	Unity of purpose Consistency of practice Collegiality and collaboration
3. A learning environment	An orderly atmosphere An attractive working environment
4. Concentration on teaching and learning	Maximisation of learning time Academic emphasis Focus on achievement
5. Purposeful teaching	Efficient organisation Clarity of purpose Structured lessons Adaptive practice
6. High expectations	High expectations all round Communicating expectations Providing intellectual challenge
7. Positive reinforcement	Clear and fair discipline Feedback
8. Monitoring progress	Monitoring pupil performance Evaluating school performance
9. Pupil rights and responsibilities	Raising pupil self-esteem Positions of responsibility Control of work
10. Home-school partnership	Parental involvement
11. A learning organisation	School-based staff development

A number of the items address, either implicitly or explicitly, the needs and interests of pupils (items 3, 4, 5, 6, 7, 8, and 9) and the right-hand column matches many of the features that pupils in our own research identify as helping them to learn. What matters is whether teachers might see, within the list, the possibility of directly involving pupils in the analysis of either the 'conditions that create undesirable experiences' (Silberman, op. cit.) or in the more detailed planning and monitoring of responses.

For guidance that takes us quite explicitly towards consultation with pupils we have to go back to the succinct list of 'performance indicators' identified by John Gray in 1990. There are only three items and the action frame in which they are presented requires pupils to provide opinions in relation to two of them. For each 'indicator' there is a question to which the school staff has to provide an answer (the five possible answers are: 'all or most'; well over half'; 'about half'; well under half'; and 'few'):

1. **Academic progress** – what proportion of pupils have made above average levels of progress over the relevant time period?

2. **Pupil satisfaction** – what proportion of pupils in the school are satisfied with the education they receive?

3. **Pupil-teacher relationships** – what proportion of pupils in the school have a good or 'vital' relationship with one or more teachers?

The problem, of course, is how to elicit reliable information, particularly in relation to question 2. Our interviews with secondary school pupils suggest that it is often more difficult to elicit information about *positive* experiences than it is about *negative* ones. (Soo Hoo also noted [1993] that 'students could not describe what meaningful learning experiences *were*, but they could describe what they *were not'*.) Gray's questions seem to be taking us in the right direction, however.

Some support for focusing on the views of the 'consumers' is offered by OFSTED: its *Framework for Inspection*, published in 1992, requires inspectors to talk with pupils about their work. 'Although this will affect the future', says Peter Lang (1993), writing about the implications of this requirement, 'there is currently little evidence that schools are paying more attention to the views of their students'. There is, however, an increasing number of researchers who are concerned about the pupil perspective, both those working within and those working outside the school improvement frame, and so we can reasonably hope that the pupil voice *may*, in time, be taken seriously as a source of insight into aspects of schooling that support and constrain young people's commitment to learning. Another important step was taken by the National Commission on Education which, in 1992, sponsored the study *What Do Students Think About Schools?* Data were gathered through questionnaire but, as Lang (1993, p. 309), reviewing the published report (by Keys and Fernandez) said: 'The problem is that [the authors] draw attention to, rather than help explain...This research is more important for the message it gives than what it actually tells us. It is a powerful reminder of the need to give students a voice'.

There are some obvious problems in legitimising the contribution of pupil voice in schools' own school improvement practices. The first is the inevitably personalised nature of the comments: pupils talk about their school, their subject teaching, their teachers; the comments are not always appreciative. In the last decade, however, the intensification of quality assurance procedures, in higher education at least, has made such evaluation proced...es more familiar if no less uncomfortable. Another problem is that policy makers, both in and outside schools, may not credit pupils with the capacity to make constructive judgements of aspects of their schooling. Meighan, for example, noted the words used by a headteacher to dismiss the idea of seeking pupils' views of teachers: 'They are not competent to judge these matters' (1977; quoted in Lang, 1993, p. 308). And Rudduck (1991), discussing the work of Wood (1988), said this:

> The problem is...that adults are so used to taking responsibility for making sense of what young people say that when opportunities are formally pro-vided in school for young people to express and explore meanings, the problems they have in communicating can be interpreted as incompetence or inability, when in fact the problems may be largely due to unreadiness – and it is our own adult behaviours that have contributed to the development of that unreadiness. (p. 50)

What researchers – and teachers who have ventured down this route – have found, however, is that young people *are* observant, *are* often capable of analytic and constructive comment, and usually respond well to the responsibility, seriously entrusted to them, of helping to identify aspects of schooling that get in the way of their learning. Our research with pupils, across schools and across a range of learning-related themes, confirms Nieto's claim for the 'depth of awareness and analysis' (p. 397) that students can offer.

Suzanne Soo Hoo recently reported an apparently successful initiative whereby students from an American 'middle school' were given the task, co-ordinated by the researcher and with support from the school, of reviewing teaching and learning; the individual experiences of the active core group were generalised through procedures which sought affirma-tion or denial from other members of the student community. One student commented:

> As I kept going to the co-researchers' meetings, I found out that other kids in our group felt the same way as I did about learning. We felt that we didn't

have much say in what we wanted to learn…We all discovered that finally we had someone who would listen to our ideas and feelings about how WE wanted to be taught.

(Angela, quoted in Soo Hoo, 1993, p. 386)

Soo Hoo echoes our own views on consulting pupils: 'Students placed in positions of responsibility and shared authority could actively investigate what was working and not working for them as learners'. She added: 'Student voices evolved as they found their experiences respected and reaffirmed by others' (ibid.). What makes the difference, it seems, is the extent to which a working relationship can be established that casts pupils as partners in a significant and continuing activity rather than as waspish critics, seizing the chance to work out their own personal vendettas. We recall the advice offered by Phelan and her colleagues, quoted earlier, that pupils should see themselves as 'co-conspirators' rather than as 'adversaries'. Wood (1988, p. 132) argues that children as young as six or seven are capable of reasoning rationally and that they can 'in some situations, transcend their own immediate perspective to appreciate what the world looks like from another point of view'. One of Soo Hoo's young co-researchers recalls the moment when she made this transition:

> The thing I remember mostly about [the co-researchers' meetings] were the group discoveries, like when it clicked in our heads that teachers were people. Students tend to think of teachers as big mean people who won't let you make up work when you're absent and can't remember your name the first week of school. But when you talk to them you learn that they have wives and kids, second jobs, boyfriends, apartments to move into, their private problems, and their own homework. Making discoveries like this is like eating dark chocolate for the first time. You remember the people and the feelings at the exact moment.

(Megan, quoted in Soo Hoo 1993, p. 392)

We would go so far as to argue that there is an educational pay-off for young people, as well as for their schools, in providing opportunities for dialogue about learning – not just dialogue about personal problems and patterns of progress but also about school structures and issues in teaching and learning.

Compared to Soo Hoo's study our own research was more concerned to build up a general picture – a pupil list of school improvement items, if you like, with supporting detail that would take teachers, parents and policy makers into their world. As Zephaniah said, 'Teachers, your students have so much to say' (1994). We talked with pupils over four years[2] but we did not go so far as Soo Hoo in casting them in the role of co-researchers and they had no sense therefore that their words were actually changing things – only that, perhaps, they might. The irony of research such as ours that operates in an action frame without being action research is that if it does make a difference to the conditions of learning in schools it is the next generation of pupils who will benefit and not those who provided the insights.

Notes

[1] This book presents data gathered in a number of different schools. In some, the term 'pupil' was regularly used and in others, 'student'. We decided in the end to use the term 'pupil' (we were also aware that books with the word 'student' in the title tend to be categorised as relating to higher education). In some references from the literature, particularly from the North American literature, the word 'student' is used and we have not, of course, attempted to standardise terms beyond the reporting of our own data.

[2] Because the study spanned several years, the research team changed its membership at several points. It was originally based at the University of Sheffield but moved with its Director, Professor Jean Rudduck, to Homerton College, Cambridge, in January 1994. The original membership of the team (in September 1991) was Dr David Gillborn, Dr Susan Harris and Professor Jean Rudduck. Dr Gillborn left after one term to take up a post at the London Institute and Professor Gwen Wallace of the University of Derby joined the team; Dr Harris left after three years to start on a new contract at the University of Sheffield and Ms Julia Day joined the team. Mrs Brenda Finney remained as the project's transcribing secretary throughout the four years; Mrs Sandra Chaplain joined the team as data manager during the last 15 months

References

Barber, M. (1994) *Urban Education Initiatives: the National Pattern*. Report for the Office for Standards in Education, University of Keele.
Gray, J. (1990) 'The quality of schooling: frameworks for judgement'. *British Journal of Educational Studies*, **38**, 3, 204–223.
Gray, J., Jesson, D., Goldstein, H., Hedger, K. and Rasbash, J. (1993) 'The statistics of school improvement: establishing the agenda'. Paper given at the ESRC seminar on School Effectiveness and School Improvement, Sheffield; published as chapter 11 in Gray, J. and Wilcox, B. (1995).
Gray, J. and Reynolds, D. (in press) 'The challenges of school improvement: preparing for the long haul', in J. Gray, D. Reynolds, C. Fitz-Gibbon and D. Jesson (eds) *Merging Traditions: The Future of Research on School Effectiveness and School Improvement*. London: Cassell.
Gray, J. and Wilcox, B. (1995) *Good School, Bad School: Evaluating Performance and Encouraging Improvement*. Buckingham: Open University Press.
Hopkins, D., Ainscow, M. and West, M. (1994) *School Improvement in an Era of Change*. London: Cassell.
Keys, W. and Fernandez, C. (1992) *What Do Students Think About School?* Report for the National Commission on Education. Slough: NFER.
Lang, P. (1985) 'Taking the consumer into account', in P. Lang and M. Marland (eds) *New Directions in Pastoral Care*. Oxford: Basil Blackwell.
Lang, P. (1993) 'Secondary students' views on school' (research review), *Children and Society*, **7**, 3, 308–313.
Louis, K. S. and Miles, M. B. (1992) *Improving the Urban High School: What Works and Why*. London: Cassell.

Meighan, R. (1977) 'Pupils' perceptions of the classroom techniques of postgraduate student teachers', *British Journal of Teacher Education*, **3**, 2, 139–148.

National Commission on Education (in press) *Success Against the Odds*. London: Routledge.

Nieto, S. (1994) 'Lessons from students on creating a chance to dream'. *Harvard Educational Review*, **64**, 4, 392–426.

OFSTED (1992) *A Framework for the Inspection of Schools*. London: Office for Standards in Education.

Phelan, P., Davidson, A. L. and Cao, H. (1992) 'Speaking up: students' perspectives on school'. *Phi Delta Kappan*, **73**, 9, 695–704.

Phelan, P., Cao, H. and Davidson, A. L. (1994) 'Navigating the psychosocial pressures of adolescence: the voices and experiences of high school youth'. *American Educational Research Journal*, **31**, 2, 415–447.

Rudduck, J. (1991) *Innovation and Change*. Buckingham: Open University Press.

Sammons, P., Hillman, J. and Mortimore, P. (1994) *Key Characteristics of Effective Schools: A Review of School Effectiveness Research*. London: Office for Standards in Education.

Schostak, J. F. and Logan, T. (1984) *Pupil Experience*. London: Croom Helm.

Silberman, M. L. (1971) 'Discussion', in M. L. Silberman (ed.) *The Experience of Schooling*. New York: Holt, Rinehart and Winston, pp. 362–364.

Soo Hoo, S. (1993) 'Students as partners in research and restructuring schools', *The Educational Forum*, **57**, Summer, 386–393.

Wood, D. (1988) *How Children Think and Learn*. Oxford: Blackwell.

Zephaniah, B. (1994) Opening lines in *Haggerston Voices*, a collection of poems written by Haggerston pupils during 1994 when Benjamin Zephaniah and Dimela Yekwai were visiting poets.

Extended note on the contributory studies

The book draws on four linked studies. The main source of data was a four-year study (1991–95) called *Making Your Way Through Secondary School*. Three specific issues raised in this core study were explored (a form of triangulation) in three 'satellite' studies. The satellite studies were all small-scale and short-term. The three issues identified were: *Disengagement and underachievement among male pupils; 'Working hard' and what it means*; and *Homework practices and gender differences*. Three secondary schools in LEAs in the North of England took part in the core study; three others from a northern LEA took part in the *Disengagement* study, one East Anglian secondary school participated in the *Homework and gender* study, and another East Anglian secondary school took part in the *Working hard* study. Overall, although there were some differences reflecting local conditions, there was remarkable similarity in pupils' views of schooling and the factors that they identified as supporting and constraining their learning, their patterns of progress and attainment, and the confidence with which they faced the future.

The core project: Making Your Way Through Secondary School: pupils' experiences of teaching and learning

The study was supported by the Economic and Social Research Council (ESRC) as part of its initiative, *Innovation and Change: The Quality of Teaching and Learning*. In planning the study we opted for a longitudinal design that would allow us to track, in real time, pupils' careers during the last four years of secondary schooling. The value of the concept 'career' to a study such as this is its 'two-sidedness': one side is linked to the development of image of self, self-identity and sense of future while the other concerns the progress of the individual through institutional time and her or his movement within the academic and social structures of the institution.

About eighty pupils have been involved in the study (the numbers fluctuate slightly as families move in and out of the localities, or as pupils are excluded from a particular school or merely choose to opt out of schooling). The pupils were 12 years old at the start of the study in 1991 (when they had just moved into year 8) and were 16 at the end. It would have been methodologically comfortable for the research team if the pupils themselves, as they progressed through years 8 to 11, were the main source of movement, with the background maintaining some stability, but this has not been so. The reforms of the 1988 Act and subsequent revisions have created a degree of turbulence – and, at times, uncertainty – in the system. Indeed, our cohort of pupils was that most closely affected by the reforms: it was in the year group that first encountered (although the pupils did not necessarily sit them) the key stage three (KS3) standard assessment tests. So, although the main focus of the research was the experiences of the young people themselves – what it is like to be a pupil in the 1990s – we had to take on a 'layered agenda', noting changes in national policy and trying to understand their impact on school identity and structures and then trying to track the impact of changes at the school level on the careers of pupils and on their sense of self-as-learner.

The research was conducted in three comprehensive schools identified by the research team as schools that were reasonably buoyant in terms of pupil numbers and generally confident about their approach and their future. They were interestingly different and were facing the challenge of change in ways that reflected their particular contexts and histories. One school was trying to shake off its former 'selective grammar school' image and it now had an economically, socially and culturally diverse pupil population. One school on the fringe of a densely populated inner urban area with fairly high levels of unemployment served a predominantly disadvantaged, working-class and ethnically mixed community but had a small influx of white middle-class parents. The third school was white and working-class and served an economically disadvantaged former coal-mining area where unemployment was also high.

After the headteachers had confirmed their interest in the project, each school managed the task of consulting/informing staff, governors, parents and pupils in ways that were consistent with its preferred style. In each school it was agreed that one year 8 class (average size, 28 pupils) would be selected by the schools for participation in the study. In all three schools, year 8 (Y8) classes were organised on mixed-ability lines although, in each, setting was either introduced or extended as a result of pressures from the National Curriculum. Each class had approximately equal numbers of boys and girls.

In each academic year three rounds of interviews were carried out with pupils (in the first year, and again at the end of the project's third year, they were interviewed in friendship pairs but otherwise the pupils were interviewed individually). Subject teachers working with pupils from the target class were interviewed once a year, while the form tutor and year tutor of the target class, the headteacher and other senior members of staff were interviewed two or three times a year. Pupil interviews lasted approximately twenty minutes while teacher interviews were usually about thirty to forty minutes long. All interviews were tape-recorded and later transcribed, coded and stored on computer. In addition, the researchers attended occasional key events affecting their target group (such as an options evening or parents' evening). The interview data were further contextualised through information gathered from the analysis of school records (including pupil reports and records of achievement) and public documents.

Data from the *Making Your Way Through Secondary School* study are presented in chapters 2, 3, 4, 5, 9, 10, 11 and 12. All but one of these chapters were written by members of the current project team (Julia Day, Jean Rudduck and Gwen Wallace). Roland Chaplain, whose research interest is stress and coping in educational settings, offered to look at the data from the pupil interviews (the nature of the stress that pupils experience in school settings has received relatively little attention) and chapter 9 is the result.

Satellite study 1: 'Working hard' and what it means

This study, reported in chapter 6, sought to explore the ways in which children understand what 'working hard' means. The research was carried out in one secondary school and three nearby primary schools. Between 21 and 24 pupils from each of years 2, 6 and 9 were interviewed individually. Here we report only the secondary school data. The pupils were selected on the basis of profiles completed by form tutors who rated pupils in terms of their tendency to 'work hard' in school and their patterns and levels of achievement. All the pupils involved were considered to be hard-working by their teachers. However, a distinction was made between pupils identified as working hard and achieving well across the curriculum and pupils identified as working hard but whose achievement was more variable. In each setting, where possible, equal numbers of female and male pupils were interviewed. In the interviews, pupils were encouraged to discuss their perceptions of themselves and of their classmates as learners. They were asked about their likes and dislikes of different aspects of school work and about how they knew whether they were doing well. They were prompted to talk about 'working hard' through reflection on their personal experiences. They were also asked about how their efforts in school were influenced by teachers and parents. The interviews were recorded and transcribed.

The fieldwork was carried out in November and December 1994 by Ruth Kershner, working with David Whitebread, Pam Pointon and Jean Rudduck.

Satellite study 2: Homework practices and gender differences

This study, reported in chapter 7, was based in an East Anglian upper school and its three 'feeder' middle schools. It set out to explore pupils' perceptions of homework and to see whether there were marked gender differences in attitude and practices. Questionnaires were designed to obtain qualitative (and some quantitative) data, with open, closed and multiple choice questions. A pilot study was carried out with 24 year 11 pupils in another school. The final version of the questionnaire was completed in December 1994 by all pupils in years 10 and 11 who were available on the day. In all, 93 girls and 101 boys in year 11 and 104 girls and 104 boys in year 10 were involved.

In addition, interviews were conducted with 54 pupils (in 18 groups of three). The interviews lasted for about twenty minutes and took place in February and March 1995. The groups were all single sex and membership was on the basis of teacher identified friendships. The sample was representative of a wide ability range. The interviews were recorded and transcribed and the content analysed.

The high profile that the research was given in the school led to considerable interest among parents. As a result, a questionnaire was issued to all year 10 parents who attended the school on three parents' evenings in March 1995 and some evidence on parent views on gender differences and homework is included in the chapter.

The research was carried out by Molly Warrington and Mike Younger.

Satellite study 3: Disengagement and underachievement among male pupils

This study, reported in chapter 8, was commissioned by a Technical and Vocational Education Extension (TVEE) consortium in the North of England which was concerned locally about what was already a national issue – disengagement and underachievement among male pupils in secondary schools.

In June and July 1994 data were collected from the three comprehensive schools in the consortium. Teachers were invited to identify boys in years 8 and 9 whom they felt were disengaged and engaged. Prior to identifying the samples the teachers were asked to provide personal constructs of pupils they considered to be disengaged. They were also invited to:

- estimate the level of disengagement among their pupils and to say when in the pupils' school careers they thought disengagement became an issue;

- say how disengagement is manifest and whether it is a general problem or limited to particular groups of pupils;
- say what they think the causes of disengagement might be.

Teachers in each school were then asked to identify two groups of boys – pupils who were seen as engaged and achieving and pupils who were seen as disengaged and underachieving. In all, 59 pupils in years 8 and 9 were involved. Of these, 32 were identified as disengaged and 27 as engaged.

Interviews were conducted in one school by three interviewers (Roland Chaplain, Sheila Miles and Jean Rudduck) using a semi-structured schedule. Each interview lasted for between 20 and 30 minutes. Pupils from the other two schools were provided with self-report questionnaires modelled on the interview schedule. The self-report questionnaires were sent directly to the schools and distributed by teachers. Anonymity was ensured by providing each respondent with an envelope which was returned, sealed, directly to the research team.

The interviews and questionnaires were designed to build a picture of how engaged and disengaged pupils perceived themselves and their learning environments. The questions probed different aspects of school life: what made pupils fed up, worried or angry; which subjects they felt they made an effort in and why; whether they thought they were treated appropriately and fairly at school; and what changes to school life might help their learning.

All three groups of pupils also completed a self-concept scale modified from an existing validated measure and each pupil's form teacher was invited to complete a modified version of an Inferred Self-Concept Scale (see notes to chapter 8 for details).

Part 1

Finding your way

Part 1 opens with pupils' recollections of setting out on the journey through secondary school. In this chapter, aptly named 'The turbulence of transition', Rudduck examines pupils' accounts of their personal and social orientation as they join the 'big school'. The pupils' comments reveal how they adjust their self-image and status in the context of encounters with new teachers, new peers and new surroundings. The chapter suggests that the social and psychological upheavals of the first few terms of secondary schooling (complicated by pupils' physical and sexual maturing) are so preoccupying that it is difficult for pupils, both individually and collectively, to focus on the seriousness of learning. Teachers in secondary schools offer imaginative and constructive support to help new pupils 'acclimatise', but our data suggest that learning is only one of many features in the exciting 'new world' of the secondary school; there are many competing and compelling rivals for pupils' attention. As pupils become familiar with the institutional routines that structure their time in school it is important that they develop internalised routines for managing learning, both on and off the school site. It is no easy task for teachers and pupils to balance the various pressures and excitements of transition in ways that allow classroom learning to have some priority.

When pupils join secondary school they have to adjust their perceptions of the role and persona of the teacher. Having had, in many cases, one teacher for most of their primary school lessons they are presented in the secondary school with a number of teachers with whom they will have a more transient relationship. In chapter 3 Wallace examines first the reactions of the younger pupils and then the perceptions of pupils who have had longer to adjust to the 'new order'. The theme of this chapter is the relationship between teachers and pupils in classrooms. It focuses on pupils' views of classroom order and the kind of teachers with whom they believe they learn best. Good teachers set clear expectations for pupil behaviour so that they know where they stand; they get to know their classes quickly, do not shout or 'go over the top', they stay calm and reasonable, and show something of themselves (their other side) to pupils. Pupils know them well enough to judge – and even to make allowances for – the mood they are in. Good teachers make it clear that they like teaching and children, they make their lessons interesting and they create a 'good classroom atmosphere'. Above all, good teachers listen to individual pupils' worries and problems and do what they can to help them through the pressures.

Chapter 4 examines the significance for pupils' learning of 'understanding' and 'not understanding'. The discussion is set in the context of the National Curriculum's early aspirations to 'coherence'. It looks at the conditions that make for 'not understanding' school work, including absence, and the problems, in pupils' words, of 'catching up' – and in ours, of building a strong scaffolding that will enable them to locate and integrate new learning. It also looks at the way that school work is given meaning by linking with pupils' frameworks of experience and interests outside school. The chapter concludes with a reminder of the fragmentation which characterises much of the structure of learning in the secondary school and the suggestion that for pupils the 'bits and pieces' they understand or don't understand within particular subjects are far more urgent and compelling than broader concerns about the curriculum as a whole.

CHAPTER 2

Going to 'the big school': the turbulence of transition[1]

Jean Rudduck

You feel like your back memories are at old school. In first year you were all for your old school. But it's your back memories now. This is like your second home.

In a book called *Inside the Secondary Classroom* (Delamont and Galton, 1986), there is a chapter on pupils' first days at a new school. It opens with an image, from a poem by Flecker, of a sinister arch – 'postern of fate…fort of fear' – that leads into the desert: 'Pass not beneath…or pass not singing', the poet advises. The same emotional tone colours the authors' commentary on pupils' move to secondary school. The school gate 'loomed…menacingly' and 'few of them felt like singing as they passed through the school entrance into what they feared might indeed be (returning to Flecker) "disaster's cavern"' (p. 43). The experience of transition presented in Delamont and Galton's book is more menacing than the experience described by pupils in our own study conducted almost ten years later.[2]

New pupils generally do experience some apprehension but it is laced with excitement and sometimes with an eager anticipation. Crossing the portal is not, now, such a momentous event: after all, pupils have usually visited the school before for induction meetings, have read the informative and welcoming documents, and a number with older sisters and brothers at the school have probably attended concerts, open evenings or sports days. Pupils may know that their new school has more resources than their primary schools, which they look forward to using, and many will experience a positive sense of leaving childish things behind now that they are going to 'the big school'. Some will also be hopeful that they can leave a reputation behind and have a fresh start. We are not claiming that transition in the 1990s is anxiety free – merely that the prospect of joining a new school is not daunting for all pupils.

In the *Making Your Way Through Secondary School* study (see chapter 1) we met our pupils for the first time at the start of year 8 (Y8) – the second year of secondary schooling. In the two schools where transfer was at 11 the period of heightened emotion, whether apprehension or excitement, had passed. We were therefore asking pupils to review their experiences of transition from a distance – when primary school had become, as one of them said, 'a back memory'. In the third school pupils moved from their primary schools a year later – a residue of the middle school system that was being gradually phased out – and here the interview comments (which we only draw on sparingly because the context is different) are more about present feelings and very recent events.

Some pupils recalled feeling a sense of loss at leaving their primary school. There, so they claimed, they knew everyone – an exaggeration perhaps but nevertheless indicative of the familiarity and security of the past. In fact, most pupils arrived at their new school with a group of young people whom they had known at their primary school and many soon started to take advantage of the opportunity to explore new friendships. The size of the new school had a powerful impact. Pupils described it as 'spacy'; they had to walk around a lot – and the walking and the new shoes could give you blisters. A particular feature of the primary school that some missed was the hall – or rather what it stood for; some had halls in which the whole school could gather and which offered a comforting sense of belonging. And when, as is not uncommon, classrooms lead off the main hall, the sense of community and safety could be even stronger. Delamont and Galton (1986) wrote about the dangers of the secondary school: some were anticipated in the myths that seem to be a standard feature of transition but some were unanticipated, such as the flames and Bunsen burners in science and the bullying that is more difficult to cope with when you are older and cannot so easily turn to your teacher for protection. And in the secondary school pupils found themselves worrying about personal property in ways that they had not anticipated. There was a different order of risk:

> ...our old school...it wasn't a small school but you still, like, in some ways you knew their name and there was no, I mean, there was no troubles, with not really people stealing anything. Just like some people took things out of lunch boxes, like a chocolate biscuit. (Y8,F)

> And that used to be a really major thing but here you can't even leave your coat or your bag in the cloakroom without getting it nicked. (Y8,F)

The loss of security showed itself in other ways. In the primary school pupils knew what to expect and how to behave, but in the new school there were some memorable occasions when they felt awkward and not in control of their environment, and their gaucheness as newcomers was exposed to others – for instance, at the first school disco:

> We ended up wearing jeans and a nice top and we wore high heels. And everyone else was in like trainers and shell suits and I just felt so out of place. (Y8,F)

Then there was the new responsibility – after spending almost all day in the one classroom – of getting to lessons on time and the painful embarrassment of turning up in the wrong place ('I stood there, white as a sheet', Y8,F) or arriving late ('I were in PE once and I never got there until about the end of the lesson. I couldn't find my way', Y8,F).

There were some other small but nevertheless important experiences of loss relating to the size and 'family' ethos of the primary school. For instance, in a small primary school all the facilities are close at hand and pupils know their way around, but in one new school the toilets seemed a long way away:

> And if you wanted to go to the toilet you had to walk right round to our common room and that's right at bottom at other end of school. (Y8, M)

And sometimes the new ways of doing things in the secondary school were complicated and difficult to understand:

> You can't take your coat or bag into the dining room at lunch time – unless you're sandwiches [and then] you *can* take your bag in [but] not your coat, so you have to leave your coat...(Y8,F)

And where homework was a new experience (see also chapter 7) it was also quite difficult to adjust to:

> Like I weren't really used to homework. I used to like not tell mum and dad about it and leave it in my bag and then I'd be doing it really late at night when I'm tired because like we didn't used to get any homework in junior school subjects then and I just didn't know what to do. (Y8,F)

The emotions that these early episodes had engendered were still etched quite sharply in pupils' minds. There was the anxiety of disorientation and the panic of being lost and late; embarrassment at the possibility of doing something foolish or childish in front of new peers and new teachers while desperately wanting to project a more adult image; and the fear of damage to possessions or even to their own bodies as a result of being the smallest in the school and therefore the 'natural' victim of careless or deliberate dominance by older pupils. Silberman rightly draws attention to the 'sheer complexity' of pupils' experiences in school; the cross-currents of transition seem to be particularly strong.

Only a very small number of pupils wished they were still at primary school. One was a pupil who had established a reputation in his new school that he was already finding it difficult to escape from:

> In old school, that's where I'd stay, me, if I had a choice. Just like go up in levels, work harder, but stay in our old school. (Y8,M)

Most, however, had settled and some had arrived at the quite sophisticated view that change is always likely to be difficult, and that it takes a while to get used to a new regime:

> If we were moving anywhere else...I'd think, 'Oh no. What's it going to be like? I won't know my way round and I won't know nobody.' 'Cos I'm used to this school, like. (Y8,M)

Alongside the vividly recollected moments of loss and embarrassment were memories of the excitements of change – 'the drunkenness of things being various' (as MacNeice put it) – and the satisfying recognition of the maturity that transfer to the secondary school symbolises. The transition myths created a certain wariness but also, for many, a kind of nervous thrill akin to the habit of peeping through your fingers at something that you are frightened of looking at directly but are too curious to miss out on. Things *do* happen – some pupils *are* thrown over the school wall or down the bank, but it usually only happens to those who court danger by being 'really cheeky to the older ones' (Y8,F). And it was also the younger ones who initiated the 'game' that was in vogue in one school. They would taunt the older pupils until they gave chase. The protagonists seemed to be evenly matched: the younger ones were smaller and generally more fleet of foot while the older ones knew their way round the school.

Many pupils found unexpected benefits in secondary school. While they were still at their primary schools they were probably unaware that they were largely confined to one classroom for most of their lessons, or that they were taught for most of the day by one teacher, for this was the norm (although it is now beginning to change). But looking back from Y8 with the wisdom of hindsight our pupils commented on the lack of variety in the primary school day (we quote from different pupils across the schools to emphasise the impact of the difference):

> You're not tied to one teacher all the time. That's what made the lower [i.e. primary] school a bit boring when you had got the same teacher all the time. (Y8,F)

> If there's a teacher you don't like you're not stuck with them for every single lesson every day of the year. (Y8,F)

> You don't have to stay in your own classroom all day...looking at same four walls. (Y8,M)

> It's better now. You can go round different lessons. It's more interesting, isn't it. Used to be just sat in one classroom like, listening to one teacher blabbering on about one thing all the time. 'Right. Now we're going to do some English, now we're going to do some maths, now we're going to do some painting'. Used to be boring. (Y8,F)

Variety can, of course, get out of hand, and one pupil recalled that in her first year she 'had, like, 32 different teachers because we like had supply teachers and we even had the school secretary once' (Y8,F).

Variety of teachers and lessons apart, there were other features of the secondary school that appealed to particular pupils, but rarely were the features directly to do with classroom learning:

> After school there's trampolining, badminton, football and things like that. (Y8,M)

> We're using nets [for basketball now] instead of just standing on chairs with our hands over our heads pretending to be baskets. (Y8,M)

> It's better equipment here and you get a better education. (Y8,M)

> 'Cos at primary school we started a quarter to nine and finished at half past three and now we start at nine and end at quarter to four. So we can stay in bed a bit longer. (Y8,F)

Other pupils liked the freedom to do what they liked during breaks and many responded positively to the more adult environment:

> When you're in junior and you come up to the secondary you can feel a difference – then when you move up to second year you can feel even more difference. They let you do more things. (Y8,F)

The interviews also revealed some areas of experience where, if pupils were not helped to develop a clear understanding of what was at stake early on, they could find later that they had unwittingly been storing up problems for themselves. One such area is absence from school and the problem of catching up on work missed; the other is homework. There are various ways in which pupils can begin to fall behind in their work. Illness apart, some are failing to build firm foundations of knowledge and practice because they are – male pupils in particular – vulnerable in class to the peer-group pressure to 'muck about'. Some are also vulnerable outside the classroom and a number of year 8 pupils recalled experiences in year 7 that made them reluctant to come to school; for example:

> Like last year one of the fifth years came bullying me and I ended up with a black eye because he wopped me round the head with his bag...I didn't want to come to school because I was scared. (Y8,M)

Another pupil talked about a friend who had a skin complaint and who now rarely came to school because she had been called names. The comment shows how easily those who do not attend school regularly get caught in a downward spiral that makes it difficult for them to catch up on work and maintain the support of their friends:

> She's quite a good worker like, but she's never here to learn. She used to be my best mate and then when she started not coming it got a bit hard because I had no one to sit with, so now we're just good friends now because she never comes. (Y8,F)

Pupils who are away for only occasional, short periods tend to use informal and somewhat *ad hoc* strategies for 'catching up'. They may, for instance, choose to copy a friend's notes, but there was no evidence to suggest that they consciously sought out, or were guided by the teacher towards, a fellow pupil who was reckoned to be good in that subject, nor that they had worried about whether or not they understood the notes they were copying. If pupils have the impression that missing work doesn't seem to be a big deal then they are likely to under-estimate the importance of the continuities of learning.[3]

A similar concern extends to homework. As we know, homework is one of the most obvious sites of quiet challenge: pupils soon learn who sets homework regularly and who marks it regularly; they see that some teachers set homework because they are obliged to and that the task they are given is not always worthwhile. And, despite the checking mechanism of the homework diary that has to be signed, pupils learn to reassure parents that either homework has not been set – when it has – or that homework has been done – when it hasn't. If the logic of homework is not respected by both teachers and pupils, or if good homework habits are not established early on in pupils' secondary school careers, it will be very difficult to adjust to the steep incline in the demands of managing time and the multiple tasks of years 10 and 11. What we are concerned about here is the onset of routine ways of thinking about learning and school work that may, in the long term, let students down.

Establishing good foundations for learning in years 7 to 9[4]

Many pupils were eager to talk about the social aspects of the new school but some pupils were also thinking about learning. One said, looking back, that what she had done in primary school wasn't 'real learning…we just used to paint and things like that' (Y8,F). Real lessons, she now claims, are things like science and doing experiments. A few complained because they were going over things they had done before in primary school but there were others, academically less sure of themselves, who were tolerant of this: they felt they would do better if they knew the work already! On the whole, pupils were expecting – and most were ready for – a new intellectual challenge, but a commitment to 'the seriousness of learning' (see Harris and Rudduck, 1993) was in tension with the novelties of the new school and with the pupils' own need to explore their new, more adult selves and relationships, both in and outside school.

Teachers in all three secondary schools put enormous effort into helping the new pupils to feel 'at home'. There were user-friendly booklets to help them find their way around. There were intensive 'social bonding' events on and off site with their new form and tutor, and there were inter-form competitions that strengthened their sense of group allegiance. But there was also the informal induction staged by older pupils which was designed, in contrast, to underline the rawness of the newcomers and their subordinate position in the pupil hierarchy. Indeed, a preoccupying concern of year 8 pupils is identity and status. It expresses itself, in part, in the pupils' reactions to teachers. At the start of secondary school they encounter a variety of teachers and this enables them to develop a critical faculty. Sometimes, as we have seen, this operates retrospectively as they re-evaluate their primary school teachers, but it also operates in the 'here and now' as they note the different styles and personalities of their current array of teachers and begin to develop strategies and tactics that enable them to assert their authority as a group. They are observing behaviours, learning to interpret moods, and judging which teachers they can safely take on in class (supply teachers, who are even newer than them, are usually a good target). All this is familiar, but it should still be emphasised that the way pupils explore and express their own power in relation to the institutional power of the teacher continues to be, on the whole, counter-productive to learning. At the same time, ironically, pupils want to learn.

It is important that schools continue to mount induction programmes in year 7 that help young people to cope with the disorientation of change and establish a sense of their membership of the school. It is also important that teachers recognise what Stenhouse called (1967, p. 131) 'the tumultuous and challenging experience' of adolescence and know how this experience (which, we suggest, has been intensified in the intervening 30 years) can distract pupils from the routines of school work. Yet pupils also need to see that learning, in terms of both content and ways of working, has continuities that are stronger than modules, terms and years, the traditional 'markers' of progress through time in secondary schooling. Distant threats (of the kind, 'If you waste time now you won't do well in your GCSEs') may have some impact but they work through coercion rather than through establishing a better understanding in young people of what the last five years of compulsory schooling are all about.

There are a number of things that teachers might do that would help to lay good foundations:

1. **Give more status to year 8**, which at present lacks the charisma and novelty of year 7 and the promise of 'ownership' that options choices offer in year 9. Year 8, by contrast, lacks a particular identity; it is a time when the dynamics of friendship groups can become all-consuming, and it may be helpful for schools to consider what particular learning-oriented characteristic could restore it. More could perhaps be made of the already prized trips and outings so that young people value them for their learning potential in addition to their social excitements and for the insights they offer into what teachers are like outside the classroom.

2. Create time for **dialogue *about* learning** alongside the time for teaching, so that pupils begin to understand the longer term implications of what they do and also begin to develop a language for thinking about learning and about themselves a learners.

3. Start **'futures' counselling in small groups** (the new guidance schemes give some support for such a move) so that young people are thinking realistically about how a commitment to learning and achievement has a long term influence on prospects and possibilities.

4. **Strengthen the procedures and practices relating to homework** (or 'extra work' since more schools are now providing opportunities for pupils to do their 'homework' at school at the end of the day). We need to recognise that young people need time to themselves out of school (even when the pressures of revision are at their most intense) but it is also apparent that unless good homework (or 'extra work') practices are established early on, many pupils will be let down by the sudden escalation of demand in years 10 and 11 and will not be able to cope. Homework is not just about pupils; the data suggest that some teachers are often unreliable in setting homework that has a clear and serious purpose and in explaining how it relates to the stage that the class has reached in a particular lesson. Some are also unreliable in responding to homework promptly. If teachers do not take it seriously pupils will pick up messages that homework doesn't matter or they will feel justifiably resentful towards those teachers whom they believe 'don't bother' to treat their work with respect. It is undoubtedly better for teachers not to set homework, or extra work, if there is nothing important to be done than to set a 'noddy' task which is then not looked at or graded. Pupils are very good at 'seeing through' such practices and 'sussing out' teachers who are acting in this way. The irony is that pupils, as the earlier chapters have shown, see such teachers as 'fair game' in the classroom but do not realise that by avoiding work with vulnerable teachers they may be making trouble for themselves in the period of preparation for their 16+ qualifications.

5. **Respond to the problem of 'catching up' for pupils who have missed work,** whether an odd day or longer periods and whether through illness or choice. If pupils gain the impression that it doesn't matter to miss sequences of learning they may find later that they do not have a strong enough scaffolding for more advanced work. Many teachers are seen to be helpful in offering advice and support but there is a problem of time and priorities. Pupils often take the initiative in copying a friend's notes, but there is no guarantee that the notes are reliable. The formalising of peer support in such situations could be an important way forward; not only would it help with the problem of work that has been missed but it would encourage pupils to articulate what has been learned and give them both a sense of responsibility and a sense of pride in the quality of their own achievement. At the moment there is a fair amount of informal peer support; pupils clearly see their peers as people they can turn to and greater use might be made of this resource.

Delamont and Galton (1986, p. 129) suggest that after the initial turmoil of joining the new school pupils are quickly 'caught up in the *normal* routine of the school year'. This is so, but it is only part of the story. The school year and the school day have their structural regularities but there are also ways of thinking about and doing school work that have to become part of individual routines, and some of those individual routines (in relation to homework, for instance) have to function outside the setting of the school. White (1971, p. 340) reminds us that institutional life is, and has to be, highly organised and that it is all too easy for the 'daily chores, the demands, the inspections' – all teacher-led and under teacher surveillance – to 'become the reality'. And so it is only when the significance of the larger purposes of schooling confront pupils – as they do in year 10 when work experience takes young people into the labour market as short term 'employees' and when the implications of not getting qualifications and not having a job hit home – that they see the importance of continuity of learning and of the build-up of reliable work habits.

As adults and as teachers it is so much easier for us than it is for pupils to see where learning is going and how important it is to establish a commitment to the seriousness of learning early on in their secondary school careers – without in any way curbing the vitality of their social exploration and their exploration of self. We do not underestimate the difficulty of learning to be a pupil.

Notes

[1] A few passages of this chapter are adapted from Harris, S and Rudduck, J (1993).

[2] Other studies of transition are discussed in Harris and Rudduck (1993). They include:

28

Nisbet and Entwistle, 1969; Power and Cotterell, 1981; Murdoch, 1982; Measor and Woods, 1984; Beynon 1985; Waterhouse, 1992.

[3]When we took pupils out of lessons to interview them we asked them how they would catch up on what they had missed; the usual responses were that it didn't matter, or that they were pleased to be missing that particular lesson, or that their friends or the teacher would tell them what they had missed.

[4]Our data on year 7 were, of course, gathered retrospectively in 1991/2 and while we recognise that in 1995 year 7 pupils may bring different experiences from their primary school into their secondary school, we do not think that this will substantially challenge our argument.

References

Beynon, J. (1985) *Initial Encounters in the Secondary School*. Lewes: Falmer Press.

Delamont, S. and Galton, M. (1986) *Inside the Secondary Classroom*. London: Routledge and Kegan Paul.

Harris, S. and Rudduck J. (1993) 'Establishing the seriousness of learning in the early years of secondary schooling'. *British Journal of Educational Psychology*, **63**, 322–336.

MacNeice, L. (1950) 'Snow' in K. Allott (ed.) *The Penguin Book of Contemporary Verse*. Harmondsworth: Penguin Books.

Measor, L. and Woods, P. (1984) *Changing Schools*. Milton Keynes: Open University Press.

Murdoch, A. (1982) *Forty-Two Children and the Transfer to Secondary Education*. (PhD thesis) Norwich: University of East Anglia.

Nisbet, J.D. and Entwistle, N.J. (1969) *The Transition to Secondary School*. London: London University Press.

Power C. and Cotterell, J. (1981) *Changes in Students in the Transition from Primary to Secondary School*. REDC Report No. 27. Canberra: Australian Government Publishing Service.

Silberman, M.L. (1971) 'Discussion', in M. L. Silberman (ed.) *The Experience of Schooling*. New York: Holt, Rinehart and Winston.

Stenhouse, L.A. (1967) *Culture and Education*. London: Nelson.

Waterhouse, S. (1992) *First Episodes: Pupil Careers in the Early Years of School*. Lewes: Falmer Press.

White, M. A. (1971) 'The view from the pupil's desk', in M. L. Silberman (ed.) *The Experience of Schooling*. New York: Holt, Rinehart and Winston.

CHAPTER 3

Relating to teachers

Gwen Wallace

She knows when to have a laugh and she knows...when she's serious.

This chapter is about the way a cohort of around eighty pupils from the *Making Your Way Through Secondary School* study (see chapter 1) described both their relationships with their teachers and the way they learned from them, over the last five years. Writing about interview data gathered from twelve year olds in a Scottish school 20 years ago, Nash (1976, p. 91) argued that the expectations pupils had of teachers influenced the teacher's behaviour. At a time when Scottish teachers routinely used 'the belt' to keep order, he showed how a teacher who wanted to change the value system and who could not keep order was seen as 'soft'. His evidence showed a teacher who was certainly ineffective in establishing order. But by explaining her ineffectiveness in terms of her different value system, rather than in terms of other aspects of her behaviour, Nash left a flaw in the analysis which throws some doubt on his thesis – and, indeed, our evidence challenges the findings. Our pupils tended to the view that it is the teachers who should set the behavioural expectations for the class, rather than the other way about. In other words, pupils did not know what to expect of particular teachers until their expectations were established. Nash's ineffective teacher was ineffective because she believed she could teach her pupils her values by verbalising them in the abstract, in a context where rules, of any kind, were left undefined, and where the teacher's behaviour did not match her expressed sentiments. Equally interesting, in the light of our data, was Nash's finding that pupils did not expect teachers to be friendly, although they regarded friendliness as a bonus. Friendliness was immensely important to our pupils; it was seen as a characteristic of teachers who, as Nash also found, were believed by pupils to like teaching and children (pp. 90–91). These teachers were, therefore, liked and respected in turn. It was this 'liking', moreover, that, in pupils eyes, led teachers to take the trouble to make their teaching interesting, to explain the work in a way that could be understood, and to be prepared to offer unstinting help when work proved difficult to get to grips with.

Given these differences, and bearing in mind the time and location of Nash's study, we need to remind ourselves how schools may have changed over the last 20 years and how different cultures view things differently. Phelan et al. (1992, p. 698) add weight to this idea. They conclude, from recent work in the United States, that 'pupils place tremendous value on having teachers who care...perhaps [as] a symptom of their loneliness and quiet desperation'.

One major change in Britain since Nash's study has been the outlawing of corporal punishment. Schools also appear to be more open places, with more parents involved as governors and (particularly in primary schools) as classroom helpers. The introduction of the National Curriculum and standardised assessment are also having an effect. Pupils' relationships with teachers may well have changed on these counts alone.

Garner (1993, pp. 405–6), writing most recently on disruptive students, has summarised the literature and concluded, 'there has been a gradual increase in awareness of the need by teachers to adopt a stance of negotiating a learning environment with the students they teach'. This sentiment is qualified by the recognition that, 'under pressure to demonstrate their effectiveness in the increasingly market-oriented environment post-ERA, there may be less willingness on the part of teachers to enter into this process'.

We now know also that schools and teachers differ in their relative effectiveness for pupils. Cooper's work (1993a, p. 133; Cooper and McIntyre, 1992; Cooper, 1993b), for example, has shown how important are an ordered, secure environment, trust between pupils and staff, mutual awareness of a shared agenda, personal involvement in learning and an understanding of the purpose of activities, together with appropriate kinds of challenge and opportunity.

We shall look further at pupils' involvement in their learning in chapter 5. Here we ask what our pupils can tell us about the way teachers establish relationships of order, security and trust in their classrooms, and how these relationships relate, in turn, to pupil learning. Finally, the data help us to understand the variations in the relative effectiveness of different teachers. We begin with an overview of the pupils' impressions after one year in secondary school. Our first round of interviews took place in September 1991 as the pupils moved into their second year of secondary schooling, year 8. Looking back over year 7, their impressions (as we saw in the last chapter) were of the variety of lessons and teachers – in contrast to their primary schools where pupils had stayed in the same room most of the day with the same teacher. In the secondary school, different teachers represented different subjects on a pre-arranged timetable.

The variety of encounters with teachers enabled pupils to extend their classification system (see Measor and Woods, 1984). They got to know which teachers they liked and disliked, which ones they found it easy to talk to and those they found difficult. Their judgements were more related to personality and style than quality of teaching and their views were consistent with other research (Beynon, 1985; Furlong, 1976; Ganaway, 1976; Woods, 1979). Towards the end of year 8, the pupils in all three schools were defining, as their ideal, teachers who would consult them, make them feel important and treat them in an adult way:

> The nicest teachers...treat you like you should be treated, not like a child or unimportant. They treat you like everybody else. They are a lot more close to us than any other teachers. (Y8,F)

However, while pupils like teachers who treat them well and who have a sense of humour, teachers have to make sure that their lessons do not get out of hand. The next section explores in more detail what our pupils told us about the way teachers establish order in their classrooms.

Establishing order, security and trust

Teaching in schools entails some kind of school and classroom order. Her Majesty's Inspectorate declares unreservedly that 'Good behaviour is a necessary condition for effective teaching and learning to take place' (OFSTED, 1993). Commonsense expectations of schooling suggest that quiet attention is the only condition under which full classroom instruction can take place and pupils need to 'settle down' if they are to 'get on with their work'. Teachers who cannot establish order seem ineffective. Pupils recognise and comment freely on such situations:

> Last year we had...[It was] really crazy...You know, you couldn't organise it unless you had everybody sat down and the teacher just couldn't do that. (Y9,F)

> It's usually lads. They keep running around, throwing paper planes, banging you over the head with books, breaking calculators that we need to use. (Y9,F)

Lacking any means of communicating effectively with pupils under such conditions, teachers who cannot 'organise it' are lost. Even teachers who can 'control' classes when facing them, may find that there is still a collective intent to disrupt their lessons which uses age-old pupil tactics: 'When the teacher turned his back everyone made a noise and when the teacher turned round everyone was quiet' (Y9,F).

Problems of classroom order were more readily described by pupils than explained. Teachers who came in as substitutes, teachers on temporary appointments and new teachers faced testing times as pupils tried to discover what they were like and what they expected pupils to do: 'Everybody takes advantage because he don't do nowt' (Y9,M). Sometimes pupils took advantage of a new teacher who knew less about the system than they did. In one case, they watched with some delight as a new teacher demonstrated that he did not know which forms to use for what purposes, particularly when issuing formal punishments. We heard, also, of teachers who, anticipating losing control, or unable to control a class, resorted to physical threats: 'He told [a pupil who talked out of turn] he was going to wipe the floor with [his] head', and some pupils reported actual instances of physical restraint. Female teachers faced with disorder were more likely to resort to verbal abuse, 'She hates our guts...She tells us to our face, "I hate you and you are bullshit, ignorant idiots"' (Y9,F).

Verbal abuse is not a tactic which succeeds. There is a depth of emotion in these encounters, as is evident in the following comments where the negative feelings are perceived as coming from the teachers; pupils feel despondent or angry:

> Hate us...Get complaints every day. They say [we're] the worst class. (Y9,F)

> The [subject] teacher always says that we are rubbish and we never do anything well. But we have been talking to the other year 9 class she teaches. She always holds them up as an example of brilliance...[But] it's not true. I don't think people will respond to it. (Y9,M)

Fortunately, teachers seeking to assert their authority or to get students to work hard by these means are relatively rare. Other problems build up around students and temporary teachers. Pupils frequently complained of the number of different teachers they had for the same subject:

> I don't do as much as I could [in the subject]...because the teachers are messing us around a bit and we keep having different teachers. We've had the teacher that came in and there's one class that was dead bad so she left or something like that, and she was only here for about a month and then she left. And then we got another teacher who's a teacher [of a different subject] originally. And then after Easter we're having another one. (Y10,M)

Finding effective ways of dealing with these problems is difficult.

Sometimes new or temporary teachers are supported by experienced staff. Classes will quieten down whenever experienced teachers come into the room only to erupt in disorder as they leave. Our schools varied in ethos and in the kind of support they gave generally to staff but there is still a tendency in some schools to leave teachers to 'sink or swim' in time-honoured professional fashion! The difference between those teachers who swam into calm and those who sank under disorder appeared to be related to three broad features of their behaviour: the survivors got to know the class quickly, they demonstrated in some ways that they liked teaching the pupils, and their expectations of pupils were generally clear and consistent ('We know where we stand with them', Y8,F). Pupils felt that they could interact in predictable ways and they had some idea of what the teacher wanted. This predictability of behaviour included staff maintaining a reliable 'balance' between inactivity in the face of pupil misdemeanours and 'going over the top'. Reactions at either extreme tended to be dysfunctional:

> She just goes over the top about everything. And she wrote on a piece of work that our class out of six was the most boring to teach and she [the teacher] didn't like it at all...and I think it just makes the class less willing to speak to her anyway. (Y9,F)

> I think a few teachers are like quite quick and they get to know the year 9s anyway. [They] like year 9s and trust them and stuff like that. I think they realise more what sort of stuff happens but some of the other teachers, I don't think they've got a clue. (Y9,M)

Given reasonably consistent patterns of behaviour from their teachers, pupils know what to expect, and can even take account of their moods.

If it was important for teachers to get to know their pupils, it was at least as important for pupils to know their teachers. School trips were useful for this because pupils found they got to know a teacher's 'other side', and responded better in class as a result. There was also a sense of give and take – a reciprocity which took some effort on the part of pupils. Where pupils felt teachers were friendly and helpful they, in turn, wanted to take the trouble to reveal something of their own better natures:

> If you get on with a teacher, you like them to get to know you, but if there's a teacher that you really don't get on with, you don't make any effort. (Y9,M)

And as three girls in year 9 put it:

> If they're prepared to treat me good, then I'll treat them good.

> She's friendly. She keeps all the class together and everything, and she's a good teacher.

> She's soft and kind – well not soft, she's nice.

Another girl described a good teacher in these words: 'You can tell her mainly everything, because she's really nice with us. She doesn't shout or anything. She is really calm and that' (Y8,F). And another said, with some feeling, 'She doesn't shout like other teachers, she just waits 'til everybody's quiet'.

It may well be significant that boys, on the whole, were less interested in the more personal dimensions of relationships than girls. A report of a study commissioned by the Mental Health Education Authority (*The Guardian*, 27/04/95), suggests that while girls want to be liked boys are more competitive and more willing to take risks in relationships. Shouting, for instance, as a means of gaining pupils' attention, appeared fairly common but while the girls tended to condemn teachers who shouted, some boys saw it as a necessary strategy for keeping them in order. Indeed, we found an occasional boy who appeared to want teachers to demonstrate their control over him, in a physical way, before he conceded legitimacy to their control.

Pupils, in general, liked teachers with a sense of humour. Used effectively, joking could be reciprocal and help to develop and maintain a degree of mutual understanding and respect. However, jokes could also be used by teachers at pupils' expense, and pupils, as we have seen above, can laugh at teachers rather than with them.

Over time, most teachers managed to negotiate an agreed order, although we shall show next how this was a part of, and not separate from, their approach to teaching; but their strategies varied. One pupil tried to find a metaphor to express the difference between classrooms that were oceans of calm and those that resembled chaos. He drew on his out-of-school experience:

> Some of the teachers can be really nasty. But then again you walk into another lesson and you know it's, like, everything changes. It's just like walking into a little nursery room with all these kids, like. Everybody's happy and then you walk into another lesson and say, 'Oh my God!' It's as though you're going into a building site. All these people. (Y10,M)

Overall, our evidence suggests that much of the 'testing out' that pupils engaged in was designed to discover the boundaries and rules of each teacher's classroom so that pupils would know what to do. Effective teachers got to know the pupils quickly and well, while sharing with pupils something about themselves, including their sense of humour. They were also clear and effective in their demands: 'She lets you have five minutes talk and then you get on with your work' (Y10,M). Even so, we will go on to show that, as pupils get older, they make judgements about the fairness and legitimacy of teachers' expectations – and react accordingly.

Teachers, trust and pupils' learning

Edward Blishen once compiled an anthology of pupils' comments on schools, taken from a competition mounted by *The Observer* in 1967. Children were invited to describe 'The School That I'd Like'. Commenting on what they had to say about discipline, he wrote: 'An unsatisfactory curriculum, dull teaching and unimaginative relationships between pupils and teachers make necessary the proliferation of petty rules' (p. 153). The charge against teachers was that they were 'teachers first, aloof authoritative persons, and ordinary companionable human beings a long way behind it all' (p. 129).

However, as we noted earlier, there have been significant changes in the last twenty years or so and our data allows us to re-examine teacher and pupil relationships as they affect learning now. In many ways they confirm Blishen's predictions. Pupils still do not take kindly to petty rules and dislike total clamp-downs on talking while they work. They dislike disorder, because they do not know where they stand, but strict teachers do not come out of our analysis well. It is difficult to use an imposed order as a means to helping pupils learn because in imposing what pupils may see as an unreasonably strict code, teachers distance themselves from the relationships necessary for productive communication. Hence, a teacher who is strict, well prepared and equipped with modern technology may not have that crucial characteristic of friendliness which enables personal engagement in interaction with pupils. Pupils are also impatient of teachers who do not explain things properly. We found, then, that pupils work on personalised views of their interactions with teachers to the extent that liking or disliking teachers is of primary significance to 'getting on well' in a subject. Such good relationships allow effective communication between teachers and pupils. They are not mere sentiment but are intimately related to the effectiveness of teaching:

> It's the change in teachers. I'm sure about that because my last teacher totally assumed I knew everything and then, when I failed, he totally had a bit of a go at me. But this teacher, he is really nice. He asks me what I know and he helps me a lot. (Y8,F)

> Mr (name) was good because he took your point of view but this year we've got Mrs (name) and I just don't like her. I get bored easily with her...On the report at the end of the year I put I thought it was good we did [this topic]. I thought it was good to learn these things and everything and I could suggest another way we could teach them...And I think she took it the wrong way and she started saying how she found our class boring. (Y8,F)

> I like Mr (name)...because he's really nice about everything and he's, I

> mean he offers to help and he says, 'Oh well come in at lunchtime if you don't understand it.' And he does it in an interesting way as well, but [our other] teacher doesn't at all. (Y9,F)

As we shall see in chapter 4, if the content of the curriculum allows for practical work this can be a bonus for teachers who want to make lessons interesting. But if the teacher talks too much and pupils cannot grasp what it is they are supposed to be doing even practical lessons will go wrong:

> In [subject] the teacher's sort of, he's really weird. He doesn't listen to you. He just walks about doing stuff and just leaves you to do everything when you don't really have the knowledge...Everything you ask, he starts sort of on this massive lecture, not lecture but this massive speech, and you don't really understand what he's talking about anyway. And so I'd have to go home and think about it. (Y9,F)

> In [subject] I don't think we've got a good teacher because the more boring it is the more they mess around because they're bored. (Y8,F)

These comments on teachers do not mean that pupils fail to see the faults in themselves. However, 'boredom' still seems to be linked to 'not understanding' or to lessons that are not interesting:

> [Science] is not the most interesting of subjects but it's just that I've never been able to grasp it and I just can't. I don't know, I've just never been able to do it. As well as finding it boring I find it difficult, so I don't try and that just puts me behind and then I just can't be bothered to do anything else. [I'm] just rubbish at the subject really. (Y10,F)

Teachers could come with very different approaches to their subject, but these were less important than the interactive relationships they established with pupils. The most successful teachers had strategies which melded their management of pupils to the content and style of their subject. Some were able to shift the mood of the class from humour to seriousness in ways which, as reported, suggested nothing less than mutually respectful relationships.

With the introduction of SATs in year 9 and the increasing importance given to grades in years 10 and 11, pupils became more concerned about teachers whom they saw as 'keeping us back' – either because they had not passed on the right information at the right time or because they had not prepared their lessons in ways that help pupils to learn:

> [I] could have done with a bit more help at the start of [my] project because he didn't give us all the information at once. It could have decided what sort of project I was going to do. (Y10,M)

> The teacher doesn't really tell us what to do. He just writes things on the board and then about five minutes later he rubs it off – and then [we] get on with it. You know, he doesn't give us the right time. We should have a sheet or something telling us what to do on it. (Y10,M)

Although some pupils were dropping out in year 10, most pupils were working for good grades and were rather more likely, at this stage, to see their learning objectively and to distinguish between syllabus, teacher and teaching:

[We] could learn more in [subject], but you can only learn so much I suppose...it's the way the topics have been set, like because the teacher was complaining that the Government have set too much in standards and things like that, so I suppose they could make it easier or just change it totally. (Y10,F)

Interestingly, finding a subject 'boring' is not at this stage a sufficient reason for not working at it. One pupil expressed a strong dislike of 'boring' poetry but was clearly learning something worthwhile about language both from the enthusiasm of his teacher and from the need to provide the required work for his GCSE portfolio:

[It's called] *November*...The first few paragraphs he describes the actual scene and the weather, then he goes into detail. He like uses really good words to describe it. And then he sees a tramp and he says he takes him for dead. Then he thinks he isn't, then he is. Then he like describes that and just describes all the landscape...It's wicked though. Do you like poetry? (Y10,M)

Pupils continued to evaluate teachers in terms of the help they gave and the extent to which they were able and willing to make lessons interesting and comprehensible, but, as we saw above, they had also learned that teachers were the source of information about examination syllabuses and grade-related standards as well as being formal assessors of their progress. This lent an added legitimacy to teacher authority, for pupils used teacher assessments as a basis for analysing their own patterns of success and failure and for shaping their work plans:

I need to get the grades. I have to have five higher grades. I need to keep my head down and work. (Y10,F)

My geography exam. That was all right. And my English is always, well it's not really marked [like] that, but the teacher's always saying, 'Oh this is really good, lovely this is, you should think about taking it further,' or whatever. (Y10,F)

Trust is a difficult concept to examine through fieldwork data. Our evidence here suggests that it is embedded in the willingness of teachers to listen to pupils and respond to their learning needs. This is a matter of communication which requires both parties to know and like each other. It seems that these needs begin to change in year 9. As pupils become more goal-oriented, they take on greater responsibility for their own progress. However, they then judge their teachers by the competence, support and encouragement they offer in relation to externally imposed demands. We suggest that it is at this period in pupils' lives that trust becomes most important. Teachers are seen by pupils as standing between them and the outside world in a way they had not appreciated in earlier years. In this sense, although pupils appear to be taking more responsibility for their own learning, they are also more dependent on teachers than they were before for information, assessment and guidance. In turning now to consider the reasons for differences in the relative effectiveness of teachers, we must bear in mind that teachers need different skills in years 7 and 8 from those required in years 10 and 11.

Difference and effectiveness

Brown and McIntyre (1993, p. 83) suggest that[6] experienced and expert teachers:

- Arrive at the class with clear goals for the pattern of activity and for the *progress* to be made by pupils.
- Make rapid initial judgements about the *conditions* impinging on the teaching, based on (a) cues which are evident on the occasion, and (b) knowledge they already have about pupils, the environment, the curriculum and themselves.
- Quickly select from their repertoire of *actions* those which their experience tells them are best suited to achieve their goals in the given *conditions*.

or alternatively modify or replace their goals.

In the light of our evidence, we can look at these activities as mirroring what pupils also do on entering classrooms. Pupils, too, come to classrooms with an agenda for action, make rapid initial judgements and select from a repertoire of possible behaviours. In this chapter we have focused on pupils' views of teachers and the way pupils learn from them. While teachers who have the ability to maintain order are likely to be seen more favourably by pupils than those who do not, the order works best where it is seen to be reasonable and well integrated with teaching methods. Pupils appreciate the trouble teachers take to make the work interesting (going off to photocopy worksheets during the lesson is definitely frowned on). It is also important to have soundly-based rules of behaviour, consistently and fairly applied, and an atmosphere where work is possible. 'Having a laugh', in mutual good humour, is still part of the deal. Good order at this level is a feature of good pupil–staff relationships and a sign of mutual respect. This is what pupils seem to imply when they talk about 'a good atmosphere' in the classroom.

However, it takes time for pupils and teachers to make the necessary relationships for effective teaching and learning and new teachers have to work exceptionally hard to establish themselves. Hence, we can understand why the experience of a succession of short-term supply teachers can undermine effective learning.

What changes the pupil–teacher relationship in years 10 and 11 is the pressure to get good grades in the 16+ examinations. As pupils begin to see their teachers as having a key information-giving and evaluative role in their own success or failure they begin to judge them accordingly. Sometimes this leads to a critical evaluation of the school or of teachers' styles of teaching (see Harris, Wallace and Rudduck, 1995); sometimes our pupils blame themselves. We might expect similar effects in the earlier years of secondary schooling as the National Curriculum and standard assessment tests become part of the institutionalised nature of schooling.

Even so, in common with Garner (1993), we found that time and again pupils emphasised the importance of interpersonal relationships with understanding teachers who were prepared to listen. Contrariwise, listening to remote and uncaring teachers 'going on and on', together with copying notes off the board and working from worksheets, were identified as features of the worst kind of lesson. Most importantly, teacher–pupil relationships, like engagement with learning (see chapter 5), carry an emotional commitment and this is likely to be reciprocal. Pupils believed that there were teachers who actively 'hated' them. Without mutual respect and caring in the relationship, pupils can feel that their efforts are futile. Our evidence reinforces the view that pupils need to feel listened to and valued by teachers if they are to achieve their full potential. It suggests that the teaching and learning relationship has emotional connotations and that successful teachers have ways of showing pupils that they like teaching – and like teaching them.

References

Beynon, J. (1985) *Initial Encounters in the Secondary School*. Lewes: Falmer Press.

Blishen E. (ed.) (undated) *The School That I'd Like*. Hammondsworth: Penguin Education Special.

Brown, S. and McIntyre, D. (1993) *Making Sense of Teaching*. Milton Keynes: Open University Press.

Cooper, P. (1993a) 'Learning from Pupils' Perspectives'. *British Journal of Special Education*, **20**, 4, 129–133.

Cooper, P. (1993b) 'Field relations and the problem of authenticity in researching participants' perceptions of teaching and learning in classrooms'. *British Educational Research Journal*, **19**, 4, 323–338.

Cooper, P. and McIntyre, D. (1992) 'Teachers' perceptions of effective classroom teaching and learning: conflicts and commonalties'. Paper presented at the annual conference of the British Educational Research Association, Stirling University, August, 1992.

Cooper, P. and McIntyre, D. (1993) 'Commonality in teachers' and pupils' perceptions of effective classroom learning'. *British Journal of Educational Psychology*, **63**, 3, 381–399.

Furlong, V. J. (1976) 'Interaction Sets in the Classroom: towards a study of pupil knowledge', in M. Hammersley and P. Woods (eds) *The Process of Schooling*. London: Routledge and Kegan Paul.

Ganaway, H. (1976) 'Making Sense of School' in M. Stubbs and S. Delamont (eds) *Explorations in Classroom Observation*. London: Wiley.

Garner, P. (1993) 'What disruptive students say about the school curriculum and the way it is taught'. *Therapeutic Care and Education*, **2**, 2, Winter, 404–415.

Guardian (1995) 'Need to be liked still blocks girls' hopes of better jobs', April 27, p. 5, London and Manchester: Guardian Newspapers.

Harris, S., Wallace, G. and Rudduck, J. (1995) ' "It's not that I haven't learnt much. It's just that I don't understand what I'm doing": metacognition and secondary school students'. *Research Papers in Education*, **10**, 2, 253–271.

Measor, L. and Woods, P. (1984) *Changing Schools*. Milton Keynes: Open University Press.

Nash, R. (1976) 'Pupils' expectations of their teachers', in M. Stubbs and S. Delamont (eds) *Explorations in Classroom Observation*. London: Wiley.

OFSTED (1993) *Education for Disaffected Pupils*. London: OFSTED Publications.

Phelan, P., Locke-Davidson, A. and Cao, H.T. (1992) 'Speaking up: students' perspectives on school'. *Phi Delta Kappan*, May, 695–704.

Woods, P. (1979) *The Divided School*. London: Routledge and Kegan Paul.

CHAPTER 4

Lessons, subjects and the curriculum: issues of 'understanding' and 'coherence'[1]

Jean Rudduck

It was suggested by HMI that, along with 'breadth and balance', 'coherence' should be one of the criteria for judging the quality of the new National Curriculum. But, as Hargreaves (1990) noted, 'somehow and for unknown reasons the concept of coherence was quietly dropped'. We can understand why! It is difficult to define and difficult to assess. For instance, coherence can be looked at from very different perspectives: there is coherence within a subject as a logic of progression building towards a meaningful 'whole'; there is coherence across subjects, where the phasing of themes and topics meshes horizontally (and also, ideally, vertically) into a generalised set of understandings; and there is the coherence that individual pupils take from the curriculum as they encounter it. It is the latter that we are interested in here. Indeed, Hargreaves (1987) suggests that coherence in the curriculum can *only* be understood in terms of *each student's* response to what the curriculum offers. According to this perspective, coherence is actively constructed rather than passively received. Pupils bring with them their own resource of experience and understanding, and coherence represents the linking of new insights, knowledge and skills into that resource; it is about 'connectedness' – how new curriculum experiences are taken on board by individual pupils – but, as our data suggest, it is also about unconnectedness.

The data are mainly from the second and third years of interviewing in the *Making Your Way Through Secondary School* study (see chapter 1), when the pupils were in years 9 and 10 and were 13 to 15 years old. It was not easy to explore directly the idea of coherence in the interviews. Instead we approached it indirectly, asking pupils about subjects they thought they were good at (or not), and why, and subjects they thought they were making good progress in (or not), and why, and we asked them what they liked and didn't like about the work in years 9 and 10. From the data we can begin to build up a picture of some dimensions of coherence in terms of the things that pupils can make sense of or understand within subjects and across subjects and the things they do not make sense of or understand. The data also allow us to begin to speculate about the reasons.

Understanding and not understanding

Not understanding

Where learning is going well 'understanding' is not something that pupils are necessarily conscious of; it is something that just happens and it is not therefore easy to articulate, but pupils do talk quite a lot in interview about 'not understanding'. Recognising that you do not understand something is generally an uncomfortable experience. Sometimes it is something quite specific that pupils cannot grasp and they seem to have a clear idea what it is they have problems in 'latching on to'. One of our pupils, for instance, who did not play an instrument, could not understand what 'notes' were in music; another was thrown by the idea of 'grids' in geography and 'square metres' in maths; and another couldn't get hold of the idea of 'circuits' in science.

More common was the experience of being 'lost' and this usually went beyond the confines of a single concept or topic and could attach to the subject as a whole – or even the curriculum as a whole. There are different reasons why pupils have such a feeling of being lost or not being able to get a grip on what is puzzling them. A common response in such a situation is to blame someone else, usually the teacher. Pupils talk about whole-class teaching with teachers who 'go too fast' or who 'don't explain things properly' and who, when pupils say that they don't understand, blame them for 'not listening' or for 'being stupid'. A pupil comments on her experience in one subject:

> In my classes I'm in a lot with people who are miles cleverer and teachers...only explain it once and I can't follow them. In maths especially like [the teacher] just explains it on the board and I don't understand what he's on about but we've got a book and it explains it as well. So me and [my friend] are reading through this book because it explains it better and by the time we've read it he's on the next chapter and we don't know what we're doing. We just get lost and everything. (Y10,F)

Another sums up the mixture of frustration and resignation that he feels when pleas for help during individual work are not met:

Like you ask him to sort out a question – like, say, if you are really stuck. You are waiting for about ten minutes and then when he comes over to you he gives you a right lecture about it. He just like goes on and on and on and then right at the end when you want to know the question he won't give it to you.

What can you do about that?

Ignore him and get on by doing it yourself. (Y9,M)

Interestingly, pupils seem to see 'coherence' and 'understanding' as something to do with the unity of approach adopted by individual teachers. Consequently, they feel that it is more difficult to make sense of what they are doing when their regular teacher is replaced by a supply teacher, or when they have more than one teacher handling the same subject. Apart from absence through illness, their regular teachers may have administrative responsibilities within the school which can take them away from lessons – 'to do somat with exams, somat like that'. One teacher, for instance, was responsible for the school computers:

He's my teacher an' all and if computers conk out he has to look after them.

And do they?

Yes, all the time. (Y10,M)

When they have supply teachers, pupils claim that they don't learn as much:

Like we're having supply teachers so us work's getting all muddled up and like some of it's getting lost like with teachers so we're having to start again [with their regular teacher] and go back over work. (Y10,M)

Work is probably 'getting lost' because pupils don't regard the work set by supply teachers as important: 'Like most of them instead of putting it in the folder just shove it in the back pocket and like forget about it and then they have to start that work again' (Y10,M). They also acknowledge that they see supply teachers as 'fair game' and in lessons taken by such teachers they accept some responsibility for the loss of time and loss of learning.

At this stage pupils usually have one teacher per subject but occasionally, where there are staffing problems, a group may have two or even three teachers simultaneously for a subject. This may be a privilege in the sixth form – although even here pupils find it difficult to adapt – but year 9 and year 10 pupils are likely to be disoriented:

I don't know whether we are getting more or less done. I think we are getting more done because we are learning three things at once. (Y9,M)

Another pupil, in a different class, comments on a similar experience:

> For [subject] I have a different teacher on a Monday and then one on Wednesday and then another on Thursday and we are all doing different subjects [i.e. topics] with each teacher so it's hard to keep up with them...The things that we are doing, like on the Monday – I don't remember what we are doing. But on Wednesday we are doing about fields and on the Thursday we are doing about...I have forgot what they call it – with all the symbols. (Y9,F)

As they get older and become aware of what is at stake in learning, pupils are less ready to 'muck about' as a group and are more ready to blame the minority of pupils who persist in playing around. Such pupils break the concentration of the group and also commandeer too much of the teacher's attention. At this stage in their school careers pupils are coming to realise that a good teacher is a precious resource in relation to understanding what they are doing:

> When we are trying to do it on our own the teacher is too busy telling people not to do stuff because there's lads in our group...banging and everything and we can't understand what he's saying and when we get it wrong he shouts at us for not getting it right, but it's not us really. (Y9,F)

Pupils would like their teachers to spend more time supporting learning and less on dealing with disruptive behaviour, but they also value time spent on careful whole-class explication of the task, the formula, the principle, or the concept, and then opportunities for individual help, with the teacher's time distributed fairly across those members of the group who want help (see Brown and McIntyre, 1993, chapter 2). The need for more individualised dialogue once the new content or task has been explained to the whole group is expressed by pupils in groups set by ability as well as by pupils in mixed-ability groups. In 'top sets' the expectation seems to be that pupils must grasp something when it is first explained: 'If you don't get it [first time] you just get left behind' (Y9,F). The pressure to 'keep up' can be considerable. In 'top sets' the work ethic may be strong but it is not easy for individual pupils to say publicly that they do not understand and they therefore appreciate opportunities for regular consultations with the teacher from which they can benefit without losing face; their alternative, if they do not understand something, is to establish a pattern of collaboration with a friend.

Sometimes, of course, it is the pupils themselves who have, over time, weakened their chances of understanding sequences of work, whether through 'mucking around in lessons' or through illness. In the Spring term interviews in year 11 a number of pupils (particularly the male pupils) said they wished they had concentrated more in earlier years because they realised now that they couldn't always make sense of what they were revising. But even during the two years of GCSE work the habit of avoiding learning is difficult to drop – as is clear from this pupil's comment, spoken with a wry recognition that she and her friends are the losers:

> Well, when we're talking we'll be talking about gossip or whatever, and when he comes to us table we'll start talking about work and then we'll talk about work with him and then it will be the end of the lesson and we've hardly done owt. (Y10,F)

As the quotations suggest, pupils were often pretty straight about their own role in disturbing the conditions for learning but they did not see what to do about their predicament:

> *Why is it that [subject] is a bit of a struggle?*
>
> Because I am not paying enough attention. Because last year I were in trouble a lot [in those lessons] so I didn't get to learn much. I just kept sulking and not paying no attention and it has all come back on me this year.
>
> *Do you think you will catch up?*
>
> Oh, no. I am too far behind. (Y9,M)

For this pupil there was in fact an escape route as the subject was one that he could drop in year 10. Another pupil, however, had had long term problems in a subject he knew was part of the core curriculum. Like the last pupil, he was finding that he had an inadequate scaffolding for learning:

> In the past I didn't used to do any [work]. They used to leave the answer books on the side so I used to just look an answer book up and copy the answers out. (Y9,M)

This pupil eventually dropped out.

Another reason why some pupils have only a limited or superficial grasp of particular sequences of learning is, of course, that they have not attended school regularly – some involuntarily through illness and others through choice. For a number of pupils in both categories the problems of catching up loom so large that the only way to deal with the dissonance is to continue to stay away. A boy whose absenteeism became more frequent during year 9 – the year when he and his peers accept that learning is really starting to matter – comments on the problem:

> *So what do you do if you stay off?*
>
> Play on the computer all day.
>
> *How do they help you catch up on what you have missed?*
>
> I've never caught up. I've always been behind. [I wasn't] too bothered about it though. But it's just starting to worry me now as I am getting older. (Y9,M)

Such pupils didn't see how they could cope when their foundations for learning were so fragile and when they knew that the work was 'getting harder'. They may, as one pupil explained, have skimmed through a series of exercises in maths in order to catch up with their peers but they then found that there were segments of the logic that they did not understand, with the result that they could not build effectively on earlier learning. Teachers in all three of our schools care about their pupils' progress and spend a lot of time checking up on absences, visiting homes, discussing the situation with pupils when they do attend and arranging for extra support in particular lessons. But, particularly in the present financial climate, resources do not allow the amount of individualised help that irregular attenders need if they are to catch up fully and take their place among their peers with self-respect and with some hope of doing well.

Sometimes a pupil will find that she or he can suddenly feel lost within a subject that, until now, they have felt comfortable with. We noticed that subjects can seem to change character quite dramatically – with a new teacher, for instance, or when pupils move into a top set and the pace changes, or when new, and usually more abstract, subject matter is introduced. The result is that pupils can quickly lose confidence and feel negative towards the subject. This can happen in languages, for instance, when the emphasis on skills work changes: one pupil wanted to drop a language because she could not cope with the intensive work on listening. It could also happen in science, when practical work in class and project 'trips' gave way to more complex learning tasks:

> I enjoy going out and that but when you come back doing things like hydrogen...God, it's hard. Because now we use diagrams like – you know, them round balls what are joined together. I don't know what they are called. We are using them now and I find it right difficult with that. (Y9,F)

Another pupil in a similar position acknowledged that she had really liked the subject she was now having difficulty with, wanted to continue with it as an option, but was 'scared' that she might 'end up not passing [at GCSE] or not doing very good because I don't understand it' (Y9,F).

We must emphasise that these were pupils who *wanted* to learn but who felt that they had little control over their own learning; they may not have believed that they had a right to press for understanding, and they may not have felt important enough to trust that teachers would respond positively if they made demands of them – especially if, in the past, they had a reputation as a 'trouble-maker'. Instead, there was a sad resignation in some of the comments: 'Want to do somat about it but we can't do owt' (Y9,M); after a period of intermittent attendance in year 10 this pupil finally dropped out completely during the first term of year 11.

Outside regular lessons, pupils are sometimes lost in the new twists and turns of the system. This was particularly true of the pupils involved in the project who were part of the national cohort destined to take the first SATs; they were, not surprisingly, bewildered by the confusion. In all the schools staff worked hard to explain the new system but the information was clearly not always easy to grasp, as this snatch of dialogue between two pupils suggests:

Well, ten's higher than a normal A.

It's like an A+.

Nine and eights are B.

Nine's an A.

It's not is it?

It is. Ten's A+, nine's A, eight and seven's – eight's B+, seven's B.

Schools also put a lot of effort into making sure that the examination itself is not too formidable but without losing the edge of awesomeness that helps pupils to focus their efforts. 'Tasters' are staged – in addition to 'mocks' – so that the experience of sitting individually in the hall (compared with being in small groups) and working silently becomes familiar (see also chapter 10). And pupils are also helped to understand the importance of reading through the questions and checking their work. One feature that teachers do not seem to have warned pupils about in these careful preparations is the fragmented nature of the examination itself. Pupils are used to working through a topic in their regular lessons but the examination papers follow a different logic, as one pupil explains, referring back to a formal 'trial' exam in geography: 'It were asking you questions – like it would go on a question on rocks and then you would turn the page and it would go on to something else, totally different' (Y10,M).

Understanding: the importance of 'connectedness'

An earlier study (see Hull et al., 1985; Rudduck, 1984) suggested that pupils rarely had much sense of the overall direction that their different courses of study were taking. Moreover, it seemed that pupils did not feel that it was necessary to know, or that they had any right to know, where lessons were heading or how they fitted together. The pupils we interviewed were, in the main, prepared to live in the present and to take lessons as they came without much concern for overall sequencing in learning. For most pupils, variety was the spice of classroom life but when they began to reflect on the seriousness of learning – as many start to do in year 9 – then they saw that security lay, to some extent, in understanding how things relate and in mastering one topic before moving on to the next.

It was noticeable that when pupils spoke about work that they had designed themselves and that they felt was very much their own – whether project work in technology or work in art – they had a strong sense of purpose, strategy and goal. When they talked about work in art, for instance, they were often articulate in explaining what they were trying to achieve. Clearly, the meaningfulness of particular tasks is greater when pupils have a degree of control over the planning and execution of the work: they have a greater sense of ownership. This is also true of topics whose content is seen to relate directly to aspects of the outside world. One pupil commented on her dislike of 'having to write things that nobody's really bothered about' (i.e. that were not really 'important') (Y9,F). Subject-based work links to the outside world in different ways; science and geography in particular made connections that were easy to grasp:

> In science we've been doing more interesting things, more like what's going on around us – like testing on animals and we are doing pollution. (Y9,F)

> And in geography we are going on the field, looking in rivers and things like that and I enjoy that. (Y9,F)

> Geography – it is like round you. (Y9,F).

> We are doing about how to use maps, about what effect weather has on rocks and all that...when we're driving down side of road and we're looking for a place, I can tell my dad where it is...where before I couldn't. (Y9,M)

In explaining her choice of social science as a year 10 option one pupil offered a string of topics that she found appealing. To us, the list – babies, first aid, surveys of people, traffic – seems incoherent but the items do have one thing in common: they are all 'things outside school' (Y9,F). A similar 'reality' criterion was used to describe what would make music better – quite simply and logically, 'to do a bit more to do with music – not just writing about it – like practising on drums and on organ and on guitars and all that, like experimenting with what you like to do' (Y9,M).

Not surprisingly, outings and trips – an obvious means of locating learning in the world outside school – score particularly high in pupils' ratings. They can last a day or a half day (for example, a visit to a local historic monument or a field trip) or, more occasionally, a week (for example, a trip abroad to take part in a musical exchange or to improve confidence in speaking a foreign language). Such events lie outside the boundary of the normal and the pressures on examination work in year 10 and year 11 mean that they are likely to feature less prominently. For teachers, such outings may be useful novelties that keep at bay the threat of pupil boredom and disengagement from learning but they can also be a powerful strategy for 'connectedness' – a means of linking school learning to the world outside school. They can also be a way of consolidating learning – an opportunity to apply what has been learned, and a time for reflecting on and seeing the relevance of a sequence of classroom work. In most cases they are highly motivating experiences with a potential for rendering understanding more concrete and meaningful.

Coherence across the curriculum

We did not gain much idea from the interviews as to whether pupils had much understanding of the curriculum as a whole. By the end of year 10 and the start of year 11, when the seriousness of learning was generally accepted, pupils' attention was drawn into their individual courses and their cross-curricular awareness was more likely to be about lack of co-ordination among teachers regarding homework and the resulting patches of intense pressure.

We did enquire, in year 9, about the functioning of the cross-curricular themes but we found that teachers were so worried about coping with the daunting and seemingly ever-changing orders in the core subjects that cross-curricularity tended to be assigned a relatively low priority. However, where work on a theme had been substantially developed, pupils recognised that they were encountering related content in different subjects. The following exchange related to work on 'environment':

> We're doing about it in science. It's...like all different environments like what the soil's like and rocks and climates and stuff like that.
>
> *And that's all in science?*
>
> We've got a bit of it in another subject because we're doing about the equator and that.
>
> *So you've got two lessons where you're doing that. Is there any link across?*
>
> Maybe, because we usually do things in pairs. Like if we're doing something in world studies we learn about the half side of it and then...we learn the other half of it in there, something like that. (Y9,F)

Another pupil also responded positively to the linkages:

At the moment we're learning in science about the ozone layer and the soil and we're doing almost the same sort of stuff in world studies...So I can relate that to each lesson, so I'm learning from one lesson and taking it to the next lesson. (Y9,M)

But although these pupils were aware of environmental issues and were enjoying the work, we could not tell whether they had, as yet, any real sense of how the different subjects offered different perspectives on the topic. Perhaps this sophistication matters less than the mere fact of their awareness and interest.

How important is coherence?

As we saw at the beginning of the chapter, the goal of 'coherence' was dropped from the specification of the national curriculum and only picked up again in terms of a network of cross-curricular themes whose impact on young people's perceptions of linkages tends to be patchy (see Rowe et al., 1993). After all, secondary schooling *is* itself fragmented – the five-year span is sharply divided into separate years, each of which has its own character; each day is divided into short, unrelated sessions; and the teaching force in any school consists of a team of people who are (for the most part) individual in approach and style. And when pupils, sensing that coherence within a subject comes from the continuity of 'their' teacher's approach, find themselves encountering more than one teacher in a subject, then 'coherence' takes another knock! Gradually, of course, pupils must learn to encounter and deal with institutional and structural variety and fragmentation and to distinguish it from epistemological continuities and coherences. But in years 9 to 11, what matters most to pupils are the bits and pieces of understanding within particular subjects or courses of study and their grasp of key procedural requirements. The data suggest, not surprisingly, that as pupils see and accept the significance of 'working hard and getting qualifications' they are even more likely to focus down on what goes on *inside* particular subjects or courses – overviews are not important to them.

A concern with overall coherence as opposed to a more focused concern about understanding aspects of work in different subjects may be an import from our adult world. We know that young children are very tolerant, in stories, of worlds that do not have the logics and constraints of the adult's world. The difference between the expectations of the child and the expectations of the adult is well caught by an American writer, Mary Alice White (1971):

The analogy that might make the student's view more comprehensible to adults is to imagine oneself on a ship sailing across an unknown sea, to an unknown destination. An adult would be desperate to know where he [*sic*] is going. But a child only knows he is going to school...The chart is neither available nor understandable to him...Very quickly, the daily life on board ship becomes all important...The daily chores, the demands, the inspections, become the reality, not the voyage, nor the destination. (p. 340)

We are aware that there are other ways of looking at coherence and understanding, other questions to be asked. We might, for instance, consider pupils' right to know where different curriculum paths are leading and whether having a working map of curriculum directions will enhance motivation. Or we might explore in greater depth the tensions between imposed frameworks and the desire of young people of 13 or 14 or so to have a greater sense of control over their own learning. There are questions about the way in which option choices are made in year 9 and whether the choices that pupils make contribute to a balanced as well as a broad curriculum. And there are also questions relating to continuities in learning and whether the ways of working experienced in schools prepare young people for ways of working outside schools. And there is another set of questions about the way that intellectual uncertainty is handled in the classroom and whether teachers 'absorb' too much of the ambiguity in the interests of presenting young people with a view of knowledge that is 'coherent' in the sense of being 'tidy'.

These are all proper concerns but we decided, in our analysis of the interview data, to focus on pupils' experience of 'understanding' and 'not understanding' their work, and how things 'fit together' within a subject, across subjects, and also in relation to work missed through non-attendance. What appears so positive from the interviews is pupils' capacity to identify what they don't understand – what it is that is leading them to feel 'lost'.

What are the implications for review of practice in schools? They are probably too obvious to spell out – and too difficult to implement because they demand more resources. The chorus of need that we see in the interviews is for more individualised support alongside clear and well-structured whole-class 'exposition'. One factor that needs highlighting in the 'class size' debate is the simple logic that if there are more pupils in a class there is less opportunity for individual help. So, the question is, recognising all the administrative and staffing pressures that schools are bearing, are there any ways in which they can make space for more individual consultation about *learning* (rather than about behaviour)? And, if so, can they legitimise the exploration of 'not understanding' so that pupils don't feel that they are 'losing face'. And can schools find

52

ways of bringing home to pupils in the earlier years of secondary schooling the importance of building good working habits (in school and at home) and a good foundation of reliable knowledge (in minds and in note-books) so that fewer pupils will experience in years 10 and 11 the dysfunctional panic of realising they are so far behind that there is little point in continuing.

Note

Some passages from this chapter were printed in an earlier paper: Rudduck, J. (1994) '"Coherence" and students' experience of learning in the secondary school', *Cambridge Journal of Education*. **24**, 2,197–211.

References

Brown, S. and McIntyre, D. (1993) *Making Sense of Teaching*. Buckingham: Open University Press.
Hargreaves, D. (1987) 'The quest for school curriculum: directions and destinations'. *School Science Review*, **69**, 126, 70–76.
Hargreaves, D. (1990) 'Planting coherence in secret gardens'. *Times Educational Supplement*, 26 January.
Hull, C., Rudduck, J. and Sigsworth, A. (1985) *A Room Full of Children Thinking: Accounts of Classroom Research by Teachers*. London: Longman, for the Schools Council.
Rowe, G. and Whitty, G. (1993) 'Five themes remain in the shadows'. *Times Educational Supplement*, 9 April, p. 8.
Rudduck, J. (1984) 'The 'hypothesis' teacher and the problem of helping children gain power through understanding', in B. Simon (ed.) *Margaret Gracie: A Teacher for our Time* (printed privately) pp. 15–23.
Silberman, M. L. (1971) 'Introduction'; 'Discussion', in M. L. Silberman (ed.) *The Experience of Schooling*. New York: Holt, Rinehart and Winston, 1–5; 362–364.
White, M. A. (1971) 'The view from the student's desk', in M. L. Silberman (ed.) *The Experience of Schooling*. New York: Holt, Rinehart and Winston, 337–345.

Part 2

Making a commitment to learning

The four chapters in Part 2 are concerned with various aspects of pupils' involvement in learning and the ways in which, faced with alternatives, they can make a commitment to learning.

Wallace's chapter considers what constitutes 'engagement' with learning in school, and the conditions that encourage and enhance on-task activity. She suggests that learning in years 7 and 8 is qualitatively different from learning in years 10 and 11, with year 9 marking a transition. She draws attention to the emotion-laden dynamics of learning, and to the different weightings pupils give to school work during the span of their secondary school careers. She documents the appeal of practical work and of lessons where pupils can take control of their learning within a framework of instruction and guidance from the teacher. Active participation in interesting work, in contrast to 'boring' routine, contributes to pupils' sense of self-development as they integrate their learning into their life-histories. Years 10 and 11 bring different priorities as pressure mounts for pupils to achieve good grades in their course work and examinations, and as instrumental purposes come to dominate the earlier meanings given to school work.

Chapter 6 explores the meaning and experience, from the pupil perspective, of 'working hard'. The exhortation to 'work hard' or the warning that next year 'you'll have to work harder' is part of a familiar teacher/parent rhetoric. The interviews in the *Making Your Way Through Secondary School* study suggested that the words had little practical meaning for pupils who, when asked, tended to explain that it merely means 'getting your head down'. Kershner took up the issue and explored it in a 'satellite' study involving younger and older pupils in one secondary school in the region and some of its 'feeder' primaries. The data from the interviews with pupils in the secondary school are discussed in this chapter. The pupils involved were judged by teachers to be among the 'hard-working' pupils in the year group; they seemed to have made a commitment to learning in the face of the distractions and difficulties that they, like all pupils, encounter in schools. These 'hard-working' pupils enjoyed school activities that allowed them some autonomy and creativity and they clearly saw education as a route to success in their future lives. They appeared to be motivated by a combination of short-term and long-term goals. Hard-working pupils are not always successful in their learning, however, and the chapter explores pupils' reactions to situations where investment of effort is not matched by good grades. Overall, the chapter suggests that it may be valuable for teachers to understand more about the different ways in which pupils recognise the experience of 'working hard', the kinds of task they are prepared to work hard at, and the different reasons they give for investing their time and thought.

One of the key differences between learning in primary and secondary schools has been the introduction of homework. Using data from the *Making Your Way Through Secondary School* study and from a satellite study in an East Anglian comprehensive school, Younger and Warrington illustrate the strong feelings that homework can generate among young people. Teachers may see homework as a means of enriching the teaching–learning process, extending and consolidating learning, promoting independent learning and research skills, and developing perseverance and self-discipline, but teachers' practices in setting and responding to homework often undermine the importance which their rhetoric ascribes to it. From a pupil's perspective, homework, by its very nature, invades leisure space, and pupils will often challenge the rights of teachers to make such claims on their independent time. The chapter also examines the extent to which reactions differ according to gender and it reflects parents' views of gender differences. The pupil voices lead the authors to suggest that schools may need seriously to review the consistency of homework policies and practices and also give thought to how they can help pupils establish, early on in the secondary school, work habits that will stand them in good stead in years 10 and 11 when the demands of school work become particularly intense.

The final chapter in Part 2 examines a topic of considerable concern: disengagement from learning among male pupils in secondary schools. This concern was reflected in the data in the *Making Your Way Through Secondary School* study and in order to extend our understanding of what is at stake in disengagement from learning a small but sharply focused 'satellite' study was carried out in three secondary schools (Chaplain, Miles and Rudduck, 1994). In this chapter, Chaplain looks at the relationship between teachers' perceptions of male disengaged pupils and the pupils' views of themselves. Teachers were asked to identify characteristics of 'disengaged' male pupils and it was notable that most descriptions related to pupils' 'inadequacies' as exemplified by disruptive behaviour, particular personality traits and difficulties beyond the control of the school. The data from the self-completion schedules, and from the interviews and questionnaires, suggested that disengaged pupils generally had less confidence than engaged pupils in their capacity to succeed; they also were more inclined to feel that teachers treated them unfairly and did not give them the help that they needed. At the same time, all the pupils involved in the study said that they wanted to achieve academically. The similarity between teachers' causal explanations for disengagement and the pupils' low sense of self-worth raises questions about the likely transmission of low expectations by some teachers to some pupils.

CHAPTER 5

Engaging with learning

Gwen Wallace

We get bored in the holidays so without school we'd be totally bored.

In this chapter we are using interview data from the *Making Your Way Through Secondary School* study (see chapter 1) to explore pupils' relationships to both the content of classroom teaching and the way it is taught. Our main analytical concept is 'engagement'; we use this term because its meaning goes beyond compliance to denote a level of emotional involvement in school work. Engagement signifies a different relationship to learning from that of 'strategic interest' explored by Woods (1980) and it focuses more closely on classroom activities than do the concerns that structure some earlier studies. We adopt it here both as a means of assessing some of the theoretical work which links engagement to learning, and as a means of highlighting the way in which pupils' feelings about curriculum content affect their learning.

Our data were collected between 1991 and 1995 and derive from interviews with parallel classes of pupils as they moved through their schooling in three very different secondary schools. Our selection of comments provides a pupil perspective on engagement over five years of schooling.

Defining engagement

As a cultural concept, engagement is more commonly associated with social relationships than with a relationship between an individual and a learning task. Used interpersonally, it carries ambiguities which make it as evocative when used with images of war and hostility as it is when associated with love, mutual trust and concern for another's well-being. In interpersonal terms, engagement is, above all, associated with strong feelings which may be positive or negative. Engagement with a task, although it implies a profound depth of involvement and interest in the subject, is also contingently related to personal and social relationships. We may engage happily with an appealing narrative, with a work of art or music, or with a task involving, for example, particular craft skills in which we take some pride. In these cases, there is a sense of personal involvement in a culturally valued activity; an identification with the task which brings some sense of satisfaction and achievement.

Yet we do not have to engage with work tasks in this way in order to carry them through. We are unlikely to feel deeply satisfied by routines that bore us, or tasks we dislike, although these may be made enjoyable by the shared company of others. We may also comply with routine demands – like vacuuming the floor or packing biscuits in a factory – for instrumental or strategic reasons. Such compliance may well ensure that the task is completed but it is unlikely to offer us a sense of achievement; rather, we often feel a sense of relief when it is finished. It is the wish to achieve the end result, rather than the satisfaction gained from engaging in the process, that has led us to act.

What then is the difference between work that engages us and work we find routine, boring or dull? We begin by examining the meaning given to the concept of engagement under the conditions in which it may occur in schools.

Wehlage et al. (1989) claim that 'engagement', although it 'no doubt occurs on a continuum...is always a prerequisite to acquiring knowledge and skills'. They go on:

> Educational engagement refers to the psychological investment...[which]...is indicated by various observable forms of student effort that demonstrate attention to, and involvement in, schoolwork. (p. 177)

The authors found that the best teaching strategies for engaging students were ones which made 'clear links with the outside world' and focused on 'contemporary events of interest and meaning to students' (p. 179). Teachers who were successful with disaffected students worked in institutions which accepted 'a proactive responsibility for educating' their young people (p. 224). 'Engagement' was best sustained, in interaction, in a supportive and interesting cultural environment which was perceived by students to offer worthwhile rewards.

Woods (1992) observed primary school pupils engaging profoundly with learning and identified such episodes as 'critical events'. Like Wehlage et al., he noted the significance of the learning support provided by the social relationships in the classroom. He argued that learning takes place best when a mutually shared understanding between teachers and pupils has been built up through 'negotiative discussion'. This occurs at different levels, over time, in a complex and developing process of co-operation.

There is much in common in these analyses. However, where Wehlage et al. stress the importance of a learning environment which offers worthwhile rewards on pupil investment, for Woods the ultimate aim for the teacher is to build a support structure for learning which enables pupils to take it over for themselves. For both, the importance of the meanings pupils give to their learning is of crucial importance. In this chapter we look at engagement in terms of the meanings our pupils gave to their learning.

The learning environment

To contextualise our pupils' perspectives it is worth recalling three significant characteristics of schools and classrooms as learning environments.

Firstly, as we have shown elsewhere (Harris, Wallace and Rudduck 1995; and chapter 3 of this volume), our pupils experienced significant changes as they moved through their secondary school careers. Initially, as they transferred from primary to secondary schooling they had to adjust to the complexity of subject timetables, with associated specialist staff. Hence, in year 7 pupils were preoccupied with settling into their new schools. This was followed by a year with little apparent focus but some exciting events, particularly in terms of school trips. In year 9 pupils were increasingly tested and differentiated into ability groupings as they were led towards options choices and urged to work harder in preparation for the examination-oriented work of years 10 and 11. Thus, while teachers of years 7 and 8 were under pressure to motivate pupils by providing work that was intrinsically interesting, teachers of years 10 and 11 were more inclined to call upon their pupils' general desire for good grades to carry them through the growing demands of coursework and examinations.

Our second point is that pupils commonly have a 'base' room where they meet collectively for registration and for lessons on personal and social education with their form tutors. However, they spend significant time during the day moving from room to room – to bases, workshops and laboratories which may include specialist equipment. On arrival they are often required to wait in corridors before entering and, on entry, must unpack relevant books and personal equipment and 'settle down'. At the end of lessons, there is a further period of 'packing up' before moving on.

These transitional states break up patterns of learning so that 'engagement' at any specific time has to be seen as a relatively short-lived event. Conventional classrooms can be restless places where pupils are slow to 'settle down'. Several pupils remarked how much easier it was to work when it was quiet; some even expressed appreciation of the absolute quiet of examination rooms. We also noted that the traditional classroom containing up to 30 pupils and one teacher remains the norm. While teachers may be able to establish and sustain a 'good atmosphere' for learning, they are sometimes working against the odds. A 'good atmosphere' for learning will be different for mathematics and drama, for science and for music, and will depend, at least to some extent, on the characteristics of the physical as well as the social environment.

To give an example: classrooms can be poorly ventilated, badly insulated and poorly heated and pupils may well be more aware of personal discomfort than they are of lesson content:

> If it's a dead hot day like this all we're doing is we're getting bunged up in classrooms...and we don't have to go outside for anything. The only time we get outside is break, dinner and home time and that's it. And all the rest we're bunged up in the building and it's dead hot and everything. (Y9,F)

Others may simply wish themselves elsewhere:

> [I long] to go home. Honestly I do. I come in and I'm going, 'Oh I just wish the day would hurry up...hurry up and pass'...I just come in and I look forward to dinner and going home and that's the only thing I look forward to. (Y9,F)

Finally, while we have noted elsewhere (see chapters 3 and 11) that significant learning can take place out of school on trips, exchanges and work placements, out-of-school learning remains the exception rather than the rule. While acknowledging that pupils generally find out-of-school activities more memorable, more engaging and more meaningful than the more usual classroom based activities, we concentrate here on engagement in classrooms.

Classrooms are teachers' territory within which pupils engage with learning on teachers' terms. Those terms change as pupils progress from year 7 to year 11 through an institutionalised process of learning upon which pupils have only marginal influence. The broad agenda is already set. Nevertheless, both teachers and pupils are active participants in an interactive situation which has physical as well as social dimensions. Importantly, pupils' own life-historical experiences and age-related characteristics influence their attitudes and behaviours and the meaning they give to their learning (see White and Brockington, 1983; Cullingford, 1991; Lang, 1993; Cooper and McIntyre, 1993).

Involvement and interest: pupils' control of learning

The first, commonsense point to make is that if pupils are to be engaged, then they need to be consciously involved as well as interested. Teachers in training are perennially urged to make their lessons interesting and our data provides insights into what interested our cohort. The comments that follow came from year 9 pupils. From this vantage point they could look back over three years of secondary schooling and tell us what had interested and involved them most:

> [A good lesson] would be interesting – [like] practicals, nothing boring. It's got to be like not very long. Can't go on for more than about three weeks or more. It's got to be fun to do...[and] you learn how to do things. (Y9,M)

In spite of Woodhead's recent (1995) exhortation to teachers to do more classroom teaching, teachers who simply talk are generally seen as boring, particularly in years 7 to 9: 'If we're doing practicals we get on with the work because we enjoy doing the practicals, but if she's talking we get bored and start talking to each other' (Y9,M). Bored pupils, particularly but not exclusively male, find alternative, more meaningful activities – as some girls in year 9 put it: 'Most of the boys like will sit in one corner and start saying stupid things and making stupid noises' (Y9,F); 'They play games at the back of the book where you make up dots...while you just carry on talking' (Y9,F). Pupils also complained about being expected to do several things at once, like copying notes from the board while listening to teachers. This suggested to us that teachers need to be sensitive as to when their interjections will be perceived as useful, or when they will distract pupils from their own thinking.

This does not mean that teacher talk, as a general activity, should be confused with the clear and effective instructions or explanations pupils need to tackle learning tasks. Given that much classroom work has, as an objective, the submission from pupils of a piece of work for assessment, it is not surprising that pupils want to know what they have to do and how they are supposed to go about it. Associated with this is the need for work to be at the right 'level'. Pupils who (in our cohort) invariably said they wanted to work hard complained about difficulties engaging with work that was 'too hard', was not fully explained or was not well understood. Occasionally this was because they had missed a lesson through absence. Teachers' responses to this often took the form of a complaint that pupils 'had not listened' or 'had not listened well enough'. It would seem sensible, therefore, for teachers to set tight limits to the amount of class-talk they do, making clear and specific what they have to say. Simple, key instructions, or outlines, in writing, at an appropriate level, could aid pupils' concentration and provide information for pupils who miss key ideas through absence.

Where the level of the task is inappropriate, problems can arise, even on programmes specifically designed to lead pupils through sequences of staged learning. Several pupils in year 9 who offered comments on the Schools Mathematics Project expressed the belief that one of the books in the series was missing and 'if you're on one too hard you need the teacher all the time'. Conversely, work could be 'too easy' and therefore 'boring'. Pupils who 'didn't understand' or who were 'bored' found the activities of their peers more interesting than lessons:

> I find it hard when you're not really...I don't know how to say this. When you're sort of not – you don't really want to do it [the work] but you're doing it because you should and then people are messing about. Like that happens in physics. You're doing work which you don't really understand which doesn't exactly fill you with enthusiasm and then people start messing about and so no one works. (Y9,F)

Some boys were rather less reluctant than this girl to admit to finding interesting alternatives to work:

> When someone else is talking and I overhear it...if it's about a favourite football team or somat, you get involved. (Y9,M)

> It's just I get distracted easily. So like I'd rather have a laugh with my friends than do maths. (Y9,M)

One pupil also explained how frustration may lead pupils to use disruptive behaviour to get the attention they believe they merit: 'I irritate [the teacher] 'til she'll help me' (Y9,F).

The positive feelings pupils have about 'practicals' was widespread. Pupils talked enthusiastically not just about doing things for themselves but also about teacher demonstrations of 'what happens if...?':

> In textiles we was doing things like burning materials and seeing which one burns quickest and things and then we was doing the warmth of the thing and how long it keeps warm for. She had a pan of water about this big and put material round it see which one lasted the longest and kept the warmest. (Y9,F)

In taking on practical tasks, pupils inevitably take over more responsibility for their own learning. In handing over significant control, teachers must accept, then, that it can go wrong. It is worth noting that pupils can learn from their failures (and those of their teachers) as well as from their successes:

> Well, I didn't do anything right. I was going crazy with the glue gun because I didn't have enough time. I had five minutes to do everything, so I just glued everything down instead of pinning it. I didn't have enough time for anything...it wasn't like they didn't give us enough time because I didn't do it right. I didn't do the proper time plan. Just taking too long on other things, just messing around talking. (Y9,M)

More conventional classroom activities may also allow pupils some degree of control. A history project on World War II was almost universally acclaimed, not simply because it was interesting, but also because pupils were encouraged to bring into school 'life-history' accounts and memories from older relatives and friends. Similar acclaim came for certain books read in English when pupils were involved in creative and imaginative work which, in association with their reading, offered both novelty and challenge:

> We do drawing, we do interesting things you know like you're trapped on a desert island and you've got to try and put all of the objects that you've got and use them to survive, and you've got to make sure that everybody survives and you've got to put them in order of use, you know, which one's more important than the other one. It's quite hard as well...We have to write up about it as well and write a big diary about what happened, which was hard. (Y9,M)

> We can work in groups and we talk about, we get in groups and we talk about like say if we want, we're on a desert, a plane's just crashed and we've got this sheet of paper and it's got all these different, you know, things that you can take with you, and you have to sort them all out into order. (Y9,F)

The book called *Smith* (Garfield, 1967) was mentioned many times by different pupils. It had involved and interested them, not just because they identified with the main character but because the teacher had used it to stretch and challenge their development through their imaginative powers. Learning which validates as well as extends pupils' personal experiences may carry such involvement over into homework:

> Some homework's okay, it's really enjoyful because we had to do a document. We read a book about Smith, 12 years old and he never had a bath for ages and that, and we did a document, because he's after a document he wants, and we did a document, made one up. (Y9,M)

It is also worth recording the response of some pupils to the way they studied *Romeo and Juliet* – one of the set texts for national assessment. Again, much of the control was handed over to them and they responded by investing their own free time in the exercise:

> There's I think there's five of us, no, six of us, doing a play of Romeo and Juliet. I'm Capula [*sic*], Leanne is Juliet, Paul's Paris and he's got four friends and they're talking about...and Paris comes to my house and [Romeo goes] to Juliet and the play just goes on from there...[We're] practising at break and dinner. (Y9,F)

In another class, pupils were drawn into imaginative experiences by the skill of the teacher in involving them in a story: 'He read to you. And it was about London, and he's from London. He's got all the accents. It was brilliant' (Y9,F).

Personal identification with the process of learning is of considerable significance. Some examples suggest how our pupils' involvement in learning gives them a sense of personal progress and growing control (the comments refer respectively to science, drama, music and mathematics):

[It's interesting because]...you can change something. Like we did one yesterday about iron sulphur. How that works is [because of] magnet[ism] in some of the iron and [we learn] how it works and that and write down. And in year 8 we're not allowed to touch it. (Y9,M)

[In drama we're learning]...how to do freeze frame and at the moment we're learning how to end a performance properly. Because most of the people say that's it; and he's going to show us how to do it properly. (Y8,F)

Well, we're playing on instruments and last year we were singing every lesson that we had with music. And [now] we're playing on the instruments and we're getting to use every instrument that we want to use or you would like to use. (Y9,F)

Well first two years we had to do little booklets so you're forever changing over. But in these you've just got one book to work through and it's more regular, you know; you know what you're doing every lesson. (Y9,F)

In each of the above cases, pupils are clearly seeing themselves as active learners, permitted to tackle increasingly more difficult tasks and developing their skills year by year. Learning has become a process which is part of their life-histories. Interestingly, girls were much more likely to relate their own development to their classroom learning than boys who felt more in control when, say, playing football. However, there were boys who also felt that they had some control over their learning in the classroom, particularly when they had the opportunity to express their own opinions: 'Bengali's been good because you can talk. We have good discussions about, you know, politics – whatever's happening' (Y9,M). Contrast this with more routine classroom work and we can see how the novelty, challenge, control over and personal identification with the task are missing when teachers limit classroom activities to routine work: 'Now sometimes in [subject] all you've got to do is reading and writing and that's it' (Y9,F).

Work where pupils had not felt in control of their learning, by definition, had little meaning and failed to engage them. The kind of learning which fell into this category was learning which was too easy or too hard, or was rendered uninteresting by what they saw as too much 'boring' teacher talk or too much 'boring' writing.

Yet although there was some general agreement on what made a good learning experience, pupils in the same class could respond quite differently to the same lesson. Sometimes we came across work that pupils strongly disliked for quite personal reasons. The source of such antagonisms did not necessarily lie within the control of the school and the following comment illustrates the way individual pupils can react in highly personal and unpredictable ways if lesson content stirs up unsuspected depths of emotion because of the personal memories it evokes:

> [In personal and social education] it was like talking about alcohol and everything and drugs and I didn't like talking about that in that lesson because it was all lesson...because my cousin died of gas. She sort of like sniffed it and she sort of like went down on her head. She died. And I didn't like it because it was too much. (Y9,F)

Form tutors are generally aware of pupils' personal circumstances. They tend to take these into account to explain or excuse particular forms of classroom behaviour. However, there are good reasons to regard personal information as confidential and there are few opportunities (even in personal and social education) to acknowledge them as valid aspects of pupils' learning. Classrooms are public arenas where private griefs tend to remain private. The implications, nonetheless, remain; pupils do not enter classrooms stripped of the emotional baggage of their own life-historical circumstances.

The growth in formal testing, the increase in differentiation by ability and the options choices pupils had to make in year 9 anticipated the changing demands of years 10 and 11. These preparations for transition into year 10 signalled changes in the locus of their social situation and affected the way they approached their school work. One pupil who acknowledged she had spent a lot of time 'messing around' indicated to us how future prospects had begun to influence her behaviour:

> [Messing around] is definitely going to stop next year because I've got to get my head down. Because if I want to get these good results and go on to college or whatever I want to do, I don't know yet, then I've got to start learning to behave and listen to what teachers are saying because if I keep on mucking about then I'm going to miss something vital and get low marks in my GCSEs. (Y9,F)

The consequences of the changing pressures varied for different pupils; many settled down in year 10 to manage their time well after some initial panic. Others, questioning the value of work which offered them little but a consciousness of failure, began to drop out. In the next section, we look at the way pupils saw their relationship to their learning change as they went through the later years of secondary schooling.

Making sense of classroom learning

Woods (1993) sees engagement as 'child-meaningful', suggesting that pupils make sense of their learning on their own terms, based on their interests. While this is reflected in our evidence from years 7, 8 and 9, our pupils showed us how they also took on board what their teachers told them about the meaning and purpose of learning, particularly as they moved into years 10 and 11. Indeed, we found that they often used teacher terms as well as reflections on their own development to make sense of their work. Importantly, this meaning-making placed both their developing sense of identity and their school learning in its wider social context – something which appeared not to happen in the earlier years. However, in placing learning in its social context, teachers defined its purpose as instrumental in shaping individual pupils' future career prospects.

The concept of 'psychological investment' (Wehlage et al.), mentioned earlier, is of relevance here. The 'investment' made by our pupils was highly individualised and related to their perceptions of an imagined future painted by their teachers. Moreover, as this goal-oriented behaviour was invoked by teachers urging their pupils to work hard for their grades in the 16+ examinations, learning for interest and satisfaction in the work itself became less significant. Hence, it was the important end grades that redefined the meaning pupils gave to their learning activities. For some pupils, lessons which did not have this kind of outcome were seen as times to 'relax' and not take work seriously. For examination subjects the effect was to add an instrumental purpose to what might otherwise appear pointless and routine. 'Getting through the syllabus' became a collective goal. As one pupil put it, teachers 'are always nagging how we must get it done...about how important it is...to get good marks' (Y10,M). Another illustrated the way externally imposed criteria gave new meaning to learning activities:

> If you're doing geography you've got to think of it as real coursework or part of the exam, so you try and do as best you can...You've got to try your best and get your best mark for them and understand it properly. (Y10,F)

For the pupils, everything now depended on the effort they, as individuals, were prepared to put into their work in order to reap the promised rewards. Pupils reacted with self-interest: 'people I used to sit with I just...used to copy off them; never used to work for myself. But now I work for myself' (Y10,F). The pressures could have the opposite effect though – and the 'lost souls' again tended to be male:

> We get a lot of pressure to do the work but, [if] because of the pressure we feel we can't do it...we sort of sidetrack. We think: 'Oh even if we do it we're not going to get any grades out of this.' We can't do it so we just mess about. (Y10,M)

There was a price to pay in year 10: 'You get more homework and more pressure'; 'it's harder work, expecting more of us and your behaviour's got to improve'; 'You've got to work quicker'; 'You get more exams and everything like tests. You have to be more mature about everything'.

Interviewed together, two boys in year 10 agreed that the way they oriented themselves to work had changed: 'I don't follow electronics at all and I don't see why we're doing it'; 'If you don't do well there's always the chance of being demoted to a lower group so you've got to keep up even if you don't like it'. This kind of comment lends weight to the behaviourist case for extrinsic reinforcement – rewards and punishments – to make pupils work more productively in school. However, we have already noted that pupils who fail to 'keep up' are likely to drop out of the game. We have also pointed out, earlier, that work done for instrumental reasons alone achieves little more than relief when the end is finally reached. We can contrast the comments we gained from pupils in year 9 about control over their learning with comments in years 10 and 11 when the rationale shifted to control over their grades.

The interviews in the spring of year 11 allowed pupils to reflect on their school careers and express their hopes and regrets. Those who felt confident of their grades appeared mature and relaxed. They generally expressed satisfaction with school and looked forward to their next step. Those who were less confident sometimes said they regretted they had not worked harder. Some said that if the pressures to work to deadlines and cope with examinations had come earlier then they might have done better. Some had given up and looked only to leaving school and getting whatever job they could. Without exception they had been surprised by how rapidly their schooldays had come to an end. With their coursework completed and only examinations to come, those who aspired to success were doing what the system required: investing their time in rote learning their notes, in preparation.

This contrasts strongly with evidence in the previous section of the kind of interest, involvement and personal control over learning some teachers managed to engender, particularly, but by no means exclusively, in years 7 to 9. Engagement then appeared as a multi-faceted concept, operating at different levels of emotion – emotion which could be positive or negative and evoked by subject content as well as by interpersonal relationships with both teachers and peers. We found it when the teaching was novel and challenging and when teachers were prepared to take risks in letting pupils take control of their learning – when pupils were caught up in an 'atmosphere' which felt right.

This suggests there may be two alternative approaches to learning in schools which make quite different demands on pupils. The first kind of engagement, engendered by school work which offers interest, novelty, challenge and significant personal control over the process, is qualitatively different from the instrumental covering of syllabuses and rote learning for examinations. These qualitative differences cannot be measured by simple test grades, for examination syllabuses may best be covered by teaching to the test. Evaluation of learning through test results disregards the importance of the kind of self-awareness of progress which pupils gain when their personal involvement in the learning task is assured. Put another way, when pupils' commitment to learning moves away from its dependence on the gratification provided in years 7 and 8 by interesting work, it becomes ever more dependent on strategies which serve their self-interest.

A flexible future?

Wehlage et al. and Woods supplied us with theories of learning based on engagement. Wehlage et al. drew on cognitive psychology and suggested that engagement, defined as pupils' 'psychological investment', was necessary for learning. Woods drew on constructivist theory to advocate an environment where pupils' learning became self-development. In the context of current institutional practices we can note that from year 10 onwards, many pupils, encouraged by teachers, consciously invest their time and energy in goal-oriented learning behaviours as a means of gaining the examination grades they need for their future careers. The environment in which they do this is one of competitive individualism. Meadmore (1993) sees this as an 'objectivising' process which produces an individuality which can be measured and controlled.

While we have powerful testimony to teachers' inventiveness and skill in engaging pupils' personal commitment to particular lessons in the first three, less pressured years, we also note the lack of overall coherence and purpose in the fragmented curriculum for these years (Rudduck, Harris and Wallace, 1994). This left teachers seeking novel ways to interest pupils, and pupils seeking immediate gratification if they were not to disengage.

As the National Curriculum and standard assessment tests engulf school work, right down to reception classes, they will supply new meaning and social purpose to school work. However, there is a danger that teachers may find themselves working with pupils in ever more instrumental ways rather than engaging them in their own 'child-meaningful' (Woods, 1993) self-development. The disadvantage of such extrinsic constraint is that it creates pressure on teachers to maintain pupils' belief in their potential to achieve worthwhile results, even when the evidence suggests otherwise (see Taylor and Wallace, 1990). While many of our pupils adapted to the pressures and demands of 16+ examinations for instrumental reasons, pupils who ceased to believe that they could get worthwhile grades tended to drop out altogether.

What is missing from the debate is that sense of social context which can help both teachers and pupils find a common social purpose as to what learning is for, rather than the strait-jacket of tests and examinations designed for an age when evidence of rote learning is viewed as the measure of high standards. As on-line computer information systems make it less and less necessary for pupils to carry information in their heads, they make it more and more necessary that pupils learn to select, analyse and 'make sense' of such information as they need it. Should school work be about learning how to learn for self-development in a social world oriented to mutual respect and support? Or is it about competitive individualism tied to individual self-interest and fragmented competencies – 'outputs' which promise (debatably) levels of achievement that can be readily measured? As we move away from the bureaucratised systems of industrialisation to the more fluid insecurities of the twenty-first century, the first option may prove to be the more appropriate.

References

Cooper, P. and McIntyre, D. (1993) 'Commonality in teachers' and pupils' perceptions of effective classroom learning'. *British Journal of Educational Psychology*, **63**, 3, 381–399.

Cullingford, C. (1991) *The Inner World of the School*. London: Cassell.

Garfield, L. (1967) *Smith*. Harmondsworth: Penguin (Puffin).

Garner, P. (1993) 'What disruptive pupils say about the school curriculum and the way it is taught'. *Therapeutic Care and Education*, **2**, 3, 404–415.

Harris, S., Wallace, G. & Rudduck, J. (1995) '"It's not that I haven't learnt much. It's just that I don't really know what I'm doing": metacognition and secondary school students'. *Research Papers in Education*, **10**, 2, 253–271.

Lang, P. (1993) 'Secondary students' views on school'. *Children and Society*, **7**, 3, 308–313.

Measor, L. and Woods, P. (1984) *Changing Schools: Pupil perspectives on transfer to a comprehensive*. Milton Keynes: Open University Press.

Meadmore, D. (1993) 'The production of individuality through examination'. *British Journal of Sociology of Education*, **14**, 1, 59–73.

Rudduck, J., Harris, S. and Wallace, G. (1994) '"Coherence" and students' experience of learning in the secondary school', *Cambridge Journal of Education*, **24**, 2, 197–211.

Taylor, J. and Wallace, G. (1990) 'Some dilemmas in implementing the criteria for continuous assessment in GCSE English'. *British Journal of Sociology of Education*, **11**, 2, 49–64.

Wehlage, G.G., Rutter, R.A., Gregory, A., Smith, N.L. and Fernandez, R.R. (1989) *Reducing the Risk: Schools as Communities of Support*. Lewes: Falmer Press.

White, R. with Brockington, D. (1983) *Tales Out of School*. London: Routledge.

Woodhead, C. (1995) *Annual Report of the Office for Standards in Education*. London: HMSO.

Woods, P. (1980) *Pupil Strategies*. London: Croom Helm.

Woods, P. (1993) *Critical Events in Teaching and Learning*. Lewes: Falmer Press.

CHAPTER 6

The meaning of 'working hard' in school

Ruth Kershner

Much of the school day takes place in classrooms and it is ostensibly devoted to 'school work' and even the vaguest pupil has some idea that you go to school to learn. Yet as one researcher put it: 'We have no direct studies of what this phenomenon "work" means to teachers and pupils'.

(Marland, 1985, citing Woods, 1978)

The need to uncover the meaning of 'schoolwork' is highlighted by the fact that pupils recognise that not only do you have to work in school but 'you have to work hard to do really well' (Y9,F).

Many of the pupils interviewed in the *Making Your Way Through Secondary School* study said that since the later years of primary school they had been told that they would have to 'work harder' as they prepared to move up to the next year group or the next school. It is as though each new step in education brings further demands on pupils. They are not just required to continue learning each year, but there is an implication that the work is going to become more difficult for them, or that the regular educational hurdles must be tackled with increasing seriousness. When pupils receive warnings or advice to work harder it is not always clear to them whether they are being required simply to increase their efforts or, more challengingly, to change their whole approach to study. There is little discussion about the reasons for working hard in school, and how to set about it. The meanings attached by pupils to 'hard work' and 'working harder' seemed, therefore, to deserve a study of their own.

A small study was set up to explore the ways in which children's understandings about 'working hard' develop through the primary and early secondary years of education. The research was carried out in one secondary school in East Anglia, and three of its feeder primary schools. Between 21 and 24 children in each of years 2, 6 and 9 were interviewed individually, using a structured schedule of questions relating to their personal experiences of learning in school. The children were encouraged to discuss their perceptions of themselves and their classmates as learners. They were asked about their likes and dislikes of different activities in school, and about how they knew whether they were doing well. They were prompted to talk about what 'working hard' meant to them, why they might think it important, and how they would set about it[1].

We chose to interview children who had all been identified by their teachers as typically 'hard workers', but who had differing levels of school achievement. Half of the group were identified by teachers as those who work hard and typically achieve well across the curriculum. The other half were those who were seen by the teachers to work hard but typically to show varying (or lower) levels of achievement. As far as possible the samples at different ages included equal numbers of boys and girls. We did not explicitly seek a balance of social and economic backgrounds, but we were aware from informal discussion with the teachers and the children that the children's family circumstances varied within the attainment groupings. In this chapter the focus is exclusively on the responses of the secondary school pupils. This group comprises 21 pupils (from three parallel year 9 classes) of whom 11 (6 boys, 5 girls) were identified as high achievers across the curriculum (h), 8 (2 boys, 6 girls) were identified as having variable achievement (v), and 2 (2 boys) were identified as typically not achieving well across the curriculum (very few pupils in the initial sample of three classes of secondary pupils were identified as typically hard-working but low achieving overall). This chapter refers primarily to the two main groups of pupils: that is, the higher achievers and those whose achievement is variable. The letters 'h' and 'v' will be used to identify the patterns of achievement of the pupils quoted, after indicating their year group (Y9) and gender (F/M).

The pupils did not know the basis for their selection but the interview data confirmed their teachers' judgements that we were indeed talking to a set of 'hard workers'. During the interviews some were identified by each other as ones who 'work very, very hard' in class. All claimed that they themselves worked at least as hard as the average in their classes, and many felt that they worked hard for most of the time in school. Several said that on occasions they were told to 'work harder' by teachers or parents, but many did not seem to need or want such direct instruction either at school or at home. In effect they were self-motivated school pupils, although, as will be discussed later, their efforts were largely maintained by the feedback that they received about their work.

When schools and pupils are faced with so many pressures, demands and problems in the current educational climate, it may seem like a luxury to ask hard-working pupils why they are working in this way. Why not leave well alone and be grateful for their efforts? It is the young people who seem unmotivated in school, and even disaffected, who are most in need of encouragement to discuss their strategies, feelings and attitudes to school work. There are, however, a large number of possible reasons why individual pupils may not work hard in school, and it is not easy to identify separate causes in a complex web of past and present experiences. One of the purposes of this research, therefore, was to explore through the pupils' eyes some of the factors that are associated with the development of confident and independent learners in school. By listening to the thoughts and feelings of pupils who are successfully matching the teachers' expectations about what it means to work hard we may hope to increase our understanding of the ways in which schools could provide an even more supportive environment, not just for the motivated and successful learners but for all pupils. As shown by the group of pupils interviewed for this study, however, effort and success in school do not necessarily go together. We therefore had a specific interest in seeing whether the well-motivated but less consistently successful pupils knew how to apply their efforts in the most effective way.

Our first concern was whether these young people would, in a short interview, be able to talk openly and analytically about school work. On the whole, we found that most of the pupils were willing and able to express their ideas and feelings, although some needed more prompting than others, and many were more articulate when talking about specific activities than general strategies or principles. The pupils were not only able to talk about their likes and dislikes regarding different subjects and teaching styles, but they could often qualify and explain their judgements in a way that showed a set of underlying educational principles. For example, one pupil was able to explain that he likes to listen to the teacher talking 'if it's of relevance...to the point'; and he likes talking to the teacher on his own 'as long as you don't spend too much time on it because that's not fair on the other people' (Y9,M,h).

The pupils' critical understanding of education was demonstrated in the way that they were able to make a distinction between school activities that were unpleasant but necessary or worthwhile, and those that seem to them to have little educational value. Few interviewees liked tests, for example, but only one questioned the need for so many (and she would accept them being longer if less frequent). In contrast, many pupils expressed a strong dislike of worksheets, for specific reasons that ranged from their blandness and repetitiveness to their unwelcome use as an activity when the usual teacher is not in school.

Many of the pupils could also talk openly about their feelings in school, distinguishing their personal responses to different activities. Several, for example, expressed a strong dislike of reading out loud to the whole class or telling the class about their work. A few said that they appreciated an audience, but others talked about being nervous, shy or embarrassed in this situation, particularly if they were not pleased with the work that they were presenting, or if they had particular concerns about their pronunciation of letters or words.

The pupils' general views about school work were explored early in the interviews, setting the context for further discussion about why, when and how they work hard in school.

Why work hard?

General views about motivation and learning

There is a continuing interest in the links between pupils' motivation to study in school, their work strategies and their attainments. Traditionally, a distinction has been drawn between motivation that is 'intrinsic' to the task in hand (such as pursuing an interest) and motivation that is 'extrinsic' (such as completing a task in order to receive a qualification) (Bruner, 1968). It has long been recognised that people will sometimes take on certain tasks primarily in order to gain the rewards at the end, but these obvious extrinsic reasons cannot account for all behaviour. There are conscious and unconscious intrinsic reasons for working, playing, eating, and carrying out any other familiar day-to-day activities; the motivation lies in the activity itself, set in its social and cultural context.

Recognition of the power of both extrinsic and intrinsic motivators in particular social settings usually means that they are used to explain why children and young people may *not* be working hard in school, rather than explaining why they do or should. For example, Wehlage et al. (1989, p. 81) identify 'impediments to educational engagement' as the absence of extrinsic rewards (like future employment) and the stifling of intrinsic rewards through a narrow conception of school learning and superficiality of curriculum 'coverage'. The assumption is often made that most school pupils would normally work acceptably hard unless there are circumstances at home or at school which prevent, hinder or distract them. Yet it is not enough to examine external factors like home background or the school curriculum in order to explain children's behaviour at school. People tend not to respond passively (or even consistently and predictably) to environmental contexts and influences, and it is important to consider the mediating effects of individual beliefs, feelings and desires (Mook, 1987), particularly people's need for recognition and acceptance by others.

Lack of motivation or effort in school may relate to individual pupils' perceptions of the likelihood of their being successful in particular tasks, or they may lie more fundamentally in the lack of value placed on school work so that even apparently strongly-motivated pupils may be depending mainly on extrinsic rewards to maintain their motivation. Some well-motivated pupils may not know how to apply themselves in the most effective way, so they are likely to have particular difficulties in maintaining their efforts in the face of disappointing results. The complexity of the issue led us to ask the pupils whom we interviewed a wide range of questions to encourage them to talk about their approaches to school work and about 'working hard', and what it entailed for them.

The pupils' views about reasons for working hard in school

All the pupils we interviewed believed that hard work at school is necessary in order to get qualifications and a good job, and to get somewhere in life. Some seemed to have been prompted to this view by the experiences of their parents, as one male pupil said of his father: 'My Dad [tells me to work harder]...I think because he had a poor education at school...[and]...he wants me to have a better one and get a good job' (Y9,M,v). A female pupil who was told to work harder by her mother (who had 'really been a trouble maker when she was at school') said: 'when my mum left school...she thinks "Well you're not just going to throw your life away and not do very well"' (Y9,F,v). In talking about long-term goals as reasons for working hard in school, many pupils seemed to be echoing the words of adults – and we heard similar views in the responses of the seven year olds and eleven year olds interviewed as part of this study (see Kershner et al., in preparation). A sizeable minority of those interviewed suggested, however, that it was necessary to have a real belief in the value of hard work; individuals had to make the decision to work hard for themselves. Some said, for example, when asked in general terms whether pupils ought to work hard in school: 'It's their own choice really, 'cos if you work hard then you've got better chances, but if you don't then you just know yourself that you are not going to do much else' (Y9,M,h). Many of the pupils' comments indicated agreement with the view that pupils in general should take heed of the future and prepare themselves: 'They think it's easy at the moment, but when they grow up they will notice how hard it is' (Y9,M,v).

The rhetoric of why pupils ought to work hard in school suggests a motivation that is more to do with extrinsic and long-term factors than with those which are intrinsic to the task in hand. This impression, however, has to be put alongside the pupils' observations that it is also important for school work to be interesting and enjoyable in its own right. 'Intrinsic' reasons for working hard in school emerged most fully when the interviewees were asked why they personally worked hard at different activities. They talked about working hardest at things they liked, things they were interested in and things that they could see a purpose for. One pupil could see that these factors were connected 'because if you are working harder, you will usually do more in the lesson and get more interested and so you'll study more for that lesson' (Y9,M,h). Other pupils made a separate connection between working hard and attainment: some worked hard at what they were already good at in order to do really well, but rather more said that they worked hard at what they found difficult in order to do better. There was some doubt that effort was enough to overcome difficulties however, because you also needed, for example, to be 'brainy' to be a lawyer (Y9,F,v) or 'good at subjects' to be a teacher (Y9,F,v). It should be noted that both of these comments came from pupils who had been judged by their teachers to have variable success within the curriculum; they seemed to be aware of the implications of the discrepancy between their efforts and their achievements and they did not believe that sheer effort would make them more successful in the long term.

There was another distinction between the pupils: those who talked mainly about long-term extrinsic motives like 'working hard to get good grades' had mostly been identified by teachers as variable or lower achievers. The 'intrinsic' motives, particularly sheer enjoyment of school activities, emerged most strongly from the pupils who were said to work hard and achieve well across the curriculum. Thankfully, perhaps, there was only one purely pragmatic reason for tackling school work with determination: 'once you've done it at least it's out the way. And it won't come back' (Y9,M,h).

One of the main findings from the interviews, therefore, was that these pupils identified both intrinsic and extrinsic reasons for working hard in school. There was an indication that the emphasis varied in relation to levels of attainment, but both types of motivation had a real presence in pupils' personal systems of beliefs and values. For many pupils, the key distinction seemed to be more to do with the personal relevance and meaning of different activities and their outcomes (short-term and long-term) than a potentially more artificial line between intrinsic and extrinsic reasons for working. There was a strong sense of personal responsibility for working and learning in school, which arose in part from identification with parents and internalisation of social and cultural values. There was also, however, a recognition that school work could be intrinsically satisfying, so teachers could be justified in emphasising the 'here and now' to control and focus learning in school, in addition to working towards the longer-term outcomes and rewards.

What is it like to work hard?

Behaviour, thought processes and feelings

Pupils are very familiar with what 'hard work' looks like. They know that other pupils are working hard because they see them in class 'with their head down'; they do not mess around or talk very much unless it is about the work; they write a lot and they get good marks. These 'hard workers' not only answer the teacher's questions, but they are also noticeable for putting their ideas forward (Y9,F,h). Some pupils distinguished between seeing other pupils as 'hard workers' and seeing them as 'clever'; one pupil analysed this in some detail when she talked admiringly about another interviewee:

> She's really clever...if we were taking notes from a video...she's got a good vocabulary and she'll be able to write it down into [her own] words ...[whereas] I'll have to write down exactly what they say...She can think of answers for everything...when we are only told to write short notes, she wrote *essays* on one thing. (Y9,F,h)

This pupil had herself been identified by teachers as well-motivated and high achieving, but she compared herself unfavourably to a classmate with such skills, and she felt that she had to 'match up to them, so if I read her piece of English then I read mine, I feel as though I have to like take some of her words and put them in mine because they sound grown up.' Pupils (especially those who are able to work collaboratively, and who may have friends with a similar orientation to school work) are strongly aware of each other's efforts and achievements, and there is almost certainly some comparison with their own standards of work and their personal knowledge of how easy or difficult it is to do well in school.

Pupils' observations of their peers are mirrored in their understanding of what they are themselves doing when they are working hard. In the eyes of all the pupils, hard work generally involves independent activity, usually best carried out in silence. There was only one interviewee who discussed working hard in collaboration with others, referring in this case to his membership of the school rugby team: 'If you're working in class, then you are just really working hard for yourself...[whereas] if you are playing sport, you'd be playing for a team' (Y9,M,h). Normally, however, hard work does not involve chatting to friends; it involves, rather, getting on independently with written work, so that more is produced and it is presented neatly and accurately. Pupils are aware of the need to concentrate and shut out distractions; one said: 'I wouldn't be able to hear things around me. I would just know the question that I was reading and the answers that I am giving in my writing book' (Y9,F,v). It is not just a matter of concentration, however, as some were aware that 'you have to use your brain more' (Y9,F,h). Working *really* hard in school, compared to normal working, is different because:

> If you are doing something in class you are usually copying something out...and it's not individual, 'cos everyone else is doing it...If you are doing your own project...it's your own ideas that you can put into practice...[when you are working really hard] you want to fulfil what your own ideas are and get them into words, all of them. (Y9,M,h)

The last two quotations are both from pupils who are high achieving, and it was noticeable that detailed comments about processes of thinking tended to be made by pupils in this group, while the pupils whose achievement was more variable overall tended to be mainly aware of behavioural signs of 'hard work', and a general need to 'concentrate'.

The pupils we interviewed were also aware of their own feelings in relation to hard work, although it was not always easy for them to explain their complex emotions. For many of them, working hard in school was associated with feelings of pride and satisfaction, especially when they knew that they had achieved something and that they might be justified in expecting praise from parents and teachers. They felt 'really good' (Y9,F,h) about their work, and when given three options of how they were most likely to feel after working hard – bored? tired? or excited? – they mostly chose 'excited'. Several commented that they also felt tired after a spell of hard work, although in some cases this may have been the result of logical reasoning rather than a strong awareness of their own feelings and experiences. As one pupil said, 'You probably get tired if you do work harder, but I think you do also feel it, well, excited, I suppose' (Y9,M,h). The fixed alternatives offered in this interview question elicited some rather dry and unconvincing answers from some interviewees, but others were led to distinguish, interestingly, work which seemed purposeful from work which seemed routine. One said, for example: 'Well, if I know I'm doing well I feel excited, but then sometimes if I *have* to do it I feel tired' (Y9,M,v). Some simply looked towards getting the routine work 'finished and done' (Y9,M,h) but several, notably from the group of high achieving pupils, got their minds 'completely concentrated and into the rhythm of things' (Y9,M,h), or even felt the kind of excitement that 'this is going to work...this is really going to be...everything really' (Y9,M,h).

For many of the pupils, the notion of hard work was closely connected with engagement in an interesting task that presented a challenge to them. The general push amongst these pupils was for more independent and creative ways of working. They spoke with pleasure about work that required them to do their own research, to use their imaginations and to make choices about what to include and what to leave out. They welcomed opportunities to put their own ideas into their work and to make it their own, even within the limits that might be set by the teacher. One girl who was enjoying writing a ballad in English said that she had to 'think of a story line...and put it into verses and...make sure the stresses are in the right places...We can make the story funny...we can have a romance, or death if we want to, you know' (Y9,F,v). Pupils talked in similar terms about a wide range of activities that included writing poetry, designing a bicycle lamp and a theatre set, researching into volcanoes, and writing the diary of a Napoleonic soldier.

Maintaining the effort

Even very young children can concentrate for a long time on interesting activities if the circumstances are right. One of the characteristics of growing up, however, is the increasing ability to concentrate at length in the face of distractions, discomfort or lack of interest. School poses particular problems for pupils of all ages with its largely imposed curriculum and a complex social and physical environment. This is one area where we might look especially to hard-working pupils to understand how they cope and maintain their efforts in this setting.

We have already seen that pupils often gained reward from engagement in a fulfilling and purposeful activity, and that they were finding some opportunities for this within the curriculum. Pupils seemed particularly to value the chance to take personal responsibility for their work, and many were prepared to spend a long time on their own projects. So while one girl spoke warmly about her regular visits to see how her cress seeds were developing, another pupil was proud of his eight hours of 'reading, writing, thinking, and also I had to do quite a lot on my presentation as well. 'Cos I did about twelve pages of A4 on it, so it was quite a long project as well' (Y9,M,h). Yet it was not only the curriculum which motivated these pupils and helped them to maintain their efforts. The pupils clearly enjoyed the opportunities for independent work, but they still felt that teachers could help them to learn. Value was placed on individualised and fine-tuned support from teachers, which was most welcome when it had been sought and received at the right time during a lesson, and preferably discreetly.

The teacher has another crucial role in helping to maintain pupils' efforts, however. Most of the pupils interviewed, at all levels of attainment, identified a strong incentive to complete tasks and receive the recognition of good marks. The question arises of whether teachers' grades and comments offer pupils anything more than a simple extrinsic reward for achievement. If this were so then pupils would become highly dependent on them, and insufficiently aware of how and why they are doing well or badly. In the light of the pupils' other comments during the interviews, however, the marks and other external signs might be interpreted, at least in part, as feedback on achievement rather than simply as rewards. The pupils had a number of sources of information about their work. They said that they knew they were doing well in their 'best' subjects because they received good marks in school or positive feedback from friends or parents. They also saw that they were in the top sets or school sports teams, or even that they were 'clapped the loudest' at public speaking (Y9,M,h). Several, too, had confidence in the value of their work. This might have been a general, unexplainable feeling that it was good (which might arise from comparison with their friends' work) or a more explicit feeling that they understood it and that 'if it's flowing, it's probably good' (Y9,M,h). In general, however, teachers' feedback and marks were important to most of the pupils interviewed, but it may be that they were not all sufficiently aware of how to use the information value of their work to identify their standards of achievement for themselves (Hastings, 1992).

The potential mismatch between effort, perceived achievement and actual feedback from teachers can cause problems for some pupils in maintaining their efforts in school. One pupil commented: 'If you get some really difficult homework, and you think you've done really well, but you haven't really, you just think "Oh well, I made an effort. I tried to do it"' (Y9,F,v). She gained satisfaction from her own knowledge that she had at least made an effort, but she did not know where to go next. Another pupil gave a different view, however: 'If something goes wrong, I don't really mind, but I feel that I should have tried harder' (Y9,F,v). This pupil got upset if things were really difficult for her in school, but had learned to deal with this feeling by not talking to anybody for a few minutes. Afterwards she felt that 'if I try hard I might be able to do it. And if I get some of the teacher's help.' These were both pupils who worked hard but whose achievement in school was variable. They had the difficult task of maintaining their motivation in the face of disappointment when they sometimes did not do well in the teacher's eyes. They differed in that the latter pupil saw a way forward when faced by work that she found difficult; she could draw both on her 'internal' resources and on the 'external' support available from her teachers. The former pupil seemed to be more accepting and less optimistic about her efforts and her achievements. Recognition of such differences between hard-working but inconsistently achieving pupils could help a teacher to offer the most appropriate guidance and support to each individual.

For pupils who do not always achieve well, the response to negative feedback about their work depends on whether they feel they could do better if they put more effort into it. In contrast, pupils who are typically high achievers across the curriculum seem more likely to be disappointed, or even surprised rather than concerned, if they receive a low mark for their work. They have more confidence in their own abilities. One female pupil said about her work that 'if I like it and I'm confident with it then I believe that I could get a good mark in it and that I'm good at it' (Y9,F,h). She could not remember many instances of being proved wrong, although she sometimes felt disappointed if she only received an 'all right' mark for something that she had spent a long time on. As another typically high achieving pupil commented: 'I suppose that deep inside I know that I'm quite good at [things], but I need a bit of confidence boosting really...but not all the time' (Y9,M,h).

These pupils' remarks about their responses to feedback in the light of their perceptions of their own efforts and abilities bring out the importance of taking account of the way that individuals think about the outcomes of their school work. Weiner (1992) has discussed the importance of pupils' own knowledge and beliefs about their level of achievement in school, not simply in terms of their responses to feedback about actual performance (as indicated by teachers' comments and grades), but, more significantly, in terms of their beliefs about the causes of their successes and apparent failures. The belief that success is due to one's own effort, for example, is likely to suggest that it is worth trying hard again in the future. In contrast, if a pupil believes that success is due to his or her natural ability, or to an unchallenging task, or to the help received from the teacher, then there may seem to be less need or value in working hard for oneself. It seems also that the learner's beliefs about the nature of the tasks set in school are a crucial link between the teacher's instructions and the pupil's decision to work. Pupils' approaches to new tasks will be influenced by their understanding of how well they responded to similar tasks in the past and why they were or were not successful. This in turn will affect their confidence about how successful they are likely to be this time, and, consequently, their eagerness to make an effort. Bandura (1981) argues that in this chain of events the most significant factor may be the learner's beliefs about the 'do-ability' of specific tasks rather than a generalised level of self-confidence about school work as a whole. As seen above, however, pupils who are typically high achievers may possess a global self-confidence about the possibility of doing well in their school work that helps to carry them through the vicissitudes of school life.

The obstacles to working hard

Knowledge about oneself as a learner is important for building up resistance to the many obstacles to learning in school, whether these arise from external or internal sources. One female pupil was not overwhelmed by what could be seen as her own weaknesses: 'If I've had a bad day or if I've got something else on my mind...then I don't work hard, but if I want to work hard I can' (Y9,F,v). In the interviews more concern was expressed about environmental factors, however. Pupils were aware of the ease with which they could be distracted by their classmates in school and this was why 'keeping your head down' was such a necessary strategy in lessons. Some calmly accepted distractions as inevitable in school ('I don't think it can really be stopped', Y9,M,h), and even recognised that they may contribute to the distractions: '[when I don't work hard]...I talk to my friends, really, and I muck about, and I get told off for talking to someone' (Y9,F,h). Simple distractions in the classroom can sometimes be magnified and given extra meaning by the prevailing peer-group culture. Our interviewees described some teasing and name-calling ('swot' in this school), but most said that this either went in phases or that it was generally dying down as they grew older. Pupils who had experienced name-calling said that they coped with it by ignoring it, and one went so far as to say, with a touch of bravado, that he regarded it as a compliment (Y9,M,h)! These pupils were forming their own judgements about the right to be independent of the crowd, and this strengthened their resolve to work hard in school. One said that at her old school she had advised a fellow pupil who was being teased for her ambition to be in the top set to 'just ignore them...what you want to do, just do it' (Y9,F,v).

The pupils were aware of another set of constraints relating to the setting in which they were expected to work. There was awareness of the limitations of the school timetable:

> Sometimes you forget things from lesson to lesson, because they're not very long, the lessons, an hour. [In] science it's only just long enough to do practical work...[and in design and technology]...you have hardly any time...and if there's not enough equipment in the classroom you have to queue up for it all the time...and then you don't always get it finished. (Y9,F,h)

Many of the pupils preferred to work at home where there was more time, space and a better atmosphere. They found it quieter and more comfortable, and they welcomed the chance to take a break when they liked. Some pupils also welcomed the resources of books and computers at home. Others had a firm preference for working in school, however, either because there were more distractions at home, like the cat and the television (Y9,F,h), or because they had other priorities after school: 'At break times and dinner times I go to the library and I do some typing or some of my homework, so that when I go home it's much more easy for me to help my parents [in their shop]' (Y9,F,v). For these pupils there was an advantage in school of having 'more people around you who are doing the same thing' (Y9,F,h), and having the teacher available to discuss things with (Y9,M,h), or simply to keep the peace: 'When you're being really noisy...they have some control over you' (Y9,F,v).

As a group, these pupils demonstrated a detailed understanding of the advantages and disadvantages of working in different social and physical settings. They could weigh up the factors that influenced their approaches to work and many showed independence of thought in their responses to the obstacles that they met. They were already resilient and positive pupils, so they did not need much encouragement to work hard in the face of obstacles, and they understood that there were some constraints (timetabling, for example) that they could not influence. However, many would have benefited from more explicit guidance about personal strategies for learning in school.

Conclusion

Why do pupils work hard?

The pupils involved in the study were beginning to exercise a personal will to learn in school. They were eager to do well in their work and they welcomed the opportunity to participate in interesting and purposeful activities. They believed in the value of education to secure qualifications and future job opportunities, but they did not conform unthinkingly to school requirements and practices. There are advantages to these multiple motivations in that they provide a number of sources of satisfaction for pupils. If a task is not interesting, for example, then the long-term view can come into play; alternatively, if pupils are distracted by friendships or they become fearful of future unemployment, then the enjoyment of a particular activity or the support of a teacher can keep them engaged.

For this group of pupils (on the whole less socially and economically disadvantaged than many of the pupils in the main study) education had become personally important, and it fitted with their lives beyond school. This is why the most salient 'extrinsic' motivators were those that were perceived to be of genuine and personal value (such as direct feedback on work or recognised qualifications that will help to gain a job in the future). It is also why the pupils talked freely about the influence of parents as well as teachers, and the experiences of learning at home as well as learning at school: the two worlds were not entirely separate for them. They felt that the world of home and the world of school were mutually supportive and provided similar goals. It must be remembered, however, that these young people had been explicitly identified as hard-working pupils. As indicated elsewhere in this book, there are also disaffected pupils in school who hold very different views about learning. Furthermore, the pupils whom we interviewed in year 9 may yet be disturbed by the pulls of the social world of young people and their own need for greater autonomy than schools normally offer. For many pupils, these factors cause a fracture between life outside school and life in school, although the two can come together again in the face of the recognised seriousness of the examination work that lies ahead of them.

It became clear in the interviews that one factor which helped pupils to maintain their motivation was the way in which they had learned to think about school and learning. Many of the pupils interviewed identified some 'bad' aspects of school without dismissing the whole thing. They may have found work difficult or uninteresting but its long-term value was not dismissed. The pupils had learned to cope with potentially difficult factors like teasing, distractions and other hindrances in the school environment. They had developed a personal resilience that could not be systematically related to single factors like gender, family background or school organisation.

Helping pupils to work harder

There are some strategies that can be employed within the school to help pupils to work hard and to learn. The focus can be on the pupils themselves, on the teaching strategies and on the structural features of the system.

The pupils

The interviews suggest that what may be important for pupils in the early years of secondary school is the opportunity to discuss learning in language which is familiar to them. There were, however, some differences between pupils which reflected their level of attainment in school. Comparatively more of the higher achieving pupils talked about intrinsic interest in school work in addition to long-term aspirations. The higher achieving pupils also had better access to their thinking and a vocabulary for talking about *how* to concentrate and study. All pupils might usefully be encouraged to discuss their aims and values, between themselves as well as with teachers, in order to extend their understanding of what education means for them and their peers. They could also be helped, particularly the variable and lower achieving pupils, to build up their understanding and control of their own learning strategies in relation to different school activities (Quicke and Winter, 1994; Hastings, 1992). The interviews support the view that in such discussions it is important to talk about approaches to work with reference to specific activities, as well as to general goals, values and strategies (this was shown, for example, in the way that the interview questions which invited pupils to give actual examples of their 'hard work' elicited more, and fuller, responses about their personal interest in school activities than did the general questions about why pupils should work hard).

The teaching strategies

The role of the teacher in planning learning, advising pupils and giving feedback about work emerges strongly in the interviews. The pupils' concern with long and short-term goals also justifies teachers' emphasis on intrinsically purposeful and worthwhile school activities alongside any reminders about the urgency of future qualifications.

One specific means of offering support to pupils in different lessons may lie in building up the motivating power of groupwork. The pupils interviewed described working hard as rather a solitary activity. They said that there were some opportunities for groupwork in school, and they liked this way of working, but it was rarely mentioned in connection with 'hard work'. Teachers could build on pupils' enjoyment of groupwork by giving more explicit feedback about group achievements and by placing emphasis on the value to individuals of this way of working (see Cowie and Rudduck, 1990).

The school system

The pupils interviewed had quite a sophisticated understanding of those aspects of the school system which obstructed their learning and those aspects which were supportive. Wehlage et al. (1989, p. 20) point out the importance of establishing pupils' sense of 'membership' of their schools, without which they are at risk of disaffection and dropping out. School membership is created through a reciprocal relationship between the pupils and the adults representing the institution; it involves active efforts by teachers to communicate with individual pupils and help them with their concerns. The pupils interviewed all had their own concerns about school, even those who were achieving well across the curriculum. Their comments showed that they had ideas about how schools should be, that they were prepared to explain their views, and that teachers could learn from consultation with them.

Note

[1] In addition to the interviews, every child carried out a short memory activity with a different interviewer. The memory tasks were included in the research to give another source of evidence about the children's abilities to apply systematic and effective strategies in their learning, and the degree to which they were aware of what they were doing. The broader findings from the whole study will be discussed elsewhere (Kershner et al., in preparation). These will be related to findings from a parallel study undertaken in Israel over the same time period (carried out by Dr. Rivka Glaubman and colleagues at Bar Ilan University, Tel Aviv). The issues and questions about 'working hard' are of international concern, and when children are being asked about why and how they should work hard, it is clearly important to consider differences in the social, political and economic context beyond the school gates.

References

Bandura, A. (1981) 'Self-referent thought: a developmental analysis of self-efficacy', in J.H. Flavell and L. Ross (eds) *Social Cognitive Development*. Cambridge: Cambridge University Press.

Bruner, J.S. (1968) *Toward a Theory of Instruction*. New York: W.W. Norton & Co. (*see particularly* chapter 6, 'The will to learn').

Cowie, H. and Rudduck, J. (1990) 'Learning from one another: the challenge', in H. C. Foot, M.J. Morgan and R.H. Shute (eds) *Children Helping Children*. Chichester: John Wiley & Sons, 235–255.

Hastings, N. (1992) 'Questions of motivation'. *Support for Learning*, **7**, 3, 135–137.

Kershner, R., Whitebread, D., Glaubman, R. and colleagues (in preparation) *What does 'working hard' mean?*. Report of a research project carried out at Homerton College, Cambridge, England and Bar Ilan University, Tel Aviv, Israel.

Marland, M. (1985) 'Our needs in schools'. In P. Lang and M. Marland (eds) *New Directions in Pastoral Care*. Oxford: Basil Blackwell.

Mook, D.G. (1987) *Motivation*. New York: W.W. Norton & Co.

Quicke, J. and Winter, C. (1994) 'Teaching the language of learning: towards a metacognitive approach to pupil empowerment'. *British Educational Research Journal*, **20**, 4, 429–445.

Wehlage, G.G., Rutter, R.A., Smith, G.A., Lesko, N. and Fernandez, R.R. (1989) *Reducing the Risk: Schools as Communities of Support*. London: Falmer Press.

Weiner, B. (1992) *Human Motivation*. London: Sage.

Woods, P. (1978) 'Negotiating the demands of schoolwork'. *Journal of Curriculum Studies*, **10**, 4, 309–27.

CHAPTER 7

Homework: dilemmas and difficulties

Molly Warrington & Mike Younger

I want it done before 'Neighbours' and 'Home and Away' start.

Homework is learning which takes place outside the context of formal classroom teaching, which is primarily the responsibility of the learner, and which is relevant to teachers' curricular objectives (MacBeath and Turner, 1990). Homework is seen by most secondary schools as important, both as an extension of the learning process and as a way of linking home and school. Indeed, Rutter (1979, p. 108) suggests that 'In some respects, the most obvious indication of a school's attitude to academic work is provided by its use of homework'. MacBeath and Turner, in their study of 13 Scottish schools, found that a school's credibility in the community was often considerably affected by its approach to homework. There are good reasons for this positive approach to the idea of homework: a number of studies have established links between the time spent on homework and academic achievement at a general level (see for example, Walberg et al., 1985; Natriello and McDill, 1986; Cooper, 1994). It is also claimed that there is an even more beneficial effect on lower achievers or working-class children (Keith, 1982; Keith and Page, 1985; Holmes and Croll, 1989).

Despite this there is, as MacBeath and Turner comment, a lack of attention given to homework in pre-service and in-service courses and in school-based staff development programmes. In fact, Wootton (1992) points out that there is often a marked difference between what school policy says should happen and what actually happens in practice, with schools' approaches to the homework problem often representing 'yet another triumph of hope over experience' (p. 3). Homework has also been relatively neglected by researchers, particularly in Britain, where only a handful of studies – such as those published by the Department of Education and Science (1987), by MacBeath and Turner (1990) and by Holmes and Croll (1989) – have focused exclusively on homework.

There has been considerably more research in the United States, partly in the context of concern over the state of American education standards (Keith et al., 1986; Miller and Kelley, 1991). These, though, have been mainly quantitative studies, designed to assess the relationship between homework and other variables on academic performance (see, for example, Paschal et al., 1984; Keith and Cool, 1992).

The focus is, however, changing, with recent British work being more orientated towards the views of the pupils, and these highlight, among other issues, a certain amount of pupil dissatisfaction with the present system of homework (Cowie and Rudduck, 1990; MacBeath and Turner, 1990; Harris and Rudduck, 1993). From a different perspective, the *Making Your Way Through Secondary School* study (MYW) (see chapter 1), in asking pupils in year 8 to look back to their first year at the school and to talk about the things that were different from their primary school, found that homework was one of the most frequently mentioned topics. Harris and Rudduck (op. cit.) have also stressed that homework is one way in which, early in pupils' secondary school careers, schools seek to communicate the seriousness of learning to pupils and their parents. They go on:

> A homework policy assigns status to schoolwork through its power to invade out-of-school zones – which pupils may see as 'leisure' zones. The status is reinforced through the apparatus of homework books which are a reminder of a formal, daily...schedule, and through the requirement that parents monitor the completion of homework and sign the book on a regular basis.

However, as the authors note, schools' efforts to encourage a commitment to learning may not always work out in practice. They show how some parents may collude, albeit unwittingly, with their children to minimise the intrusion of school work into their 'own time'. Some year 7 pupils, seeing homework as an exciting novelty, are devout in their pursuit of what their teachers ask them to do, while others learn that it is not always treated as seriously as their teachers have led them to believe it should be.

This chapter draws upon data from the MYW study, but extends it with material from an in-depth study of an East Anglian comprehensive school. The East Anglian study grew out of a recognition of the need to look in greater detail at some issues raised in the early phase of the MYW study. The MYW study did not gather data from parents, only *about* parents, incidentally, through pupil comments, and yet, as that study recognised, the role of parents is an important aspect of the homework process. The importance of this role is reinforced by the final interviews in the MYW study, which underline the importance of establishing good working habits both in and outside school. Secondly, in a context of apparent underachievement by male pupils at a national level, the MYW interviews began to explore female and male attitudes to school and homework. Harris, Nixon and Rudduck (1993) point out the existence of a gender 'regime' in the community, influencing pupils' homework practices. They found that, while girls were more ready to do school work at home, planning their work and discussing it with close friends, boys seemed less committed to working regularly, preferring to spend time out of school in large groups of their own sex, often engaged in sporting activities.

The East Anglian study was thus designed to look more closely at the way in which approaches to homework are gendered. Like the MYW project, our work focused on the pupils themselves, examining their views and perspectives on homework, but it also took into account parental opinions. The fieldwork for the first phase of this project (which is reported here) was carried out between November 1994 and March 1995, at a co-educational state upper school (for pupils from years 13 to 18) and its two feeder middle schools. The upper school is situated in a mainly rural area, with some affluent commuter housing, but with a large proportion of the catchment area consisting of local authority housing; the pupil intake is therefore mixed. It was established in the early 1970s, when schools in the area were organised along comprehensive lines, and now caters for around a thousand pupils, of whom about one third are in the sixth form. The data on which this chapter is based comes from questionnaires completed by 197 girls and 205 boys in years 10 and 11, from 36 girls and 35 boys in year 8 in the two middle schools, and from interviews with 18 groups of years 10 and 11 pupils. Questionnaires were also completed by parents of 50 year 10 girls and 44 year 10 boys. For a description of the methodology used, the reader is referred to chapter 1.

Pupil perspectives on homework

Given the evidence cited above, that time spent on homework can have beneficial effects on academic achievement, it would seem important that it is seen by the pupils to have a purpose, that it is well organised, and that it is manageable. Discussion in the interviews in both projects, however, was often concerned with these very issues, with pupils questioning the rationale for homework itself, criticising the organisation and nature of the set tasks, and finding it difficult to reconcile the demands of homework with other extra-curricular activities. This section of the chapter explores these topics and the effects which they have on pupil motivation to get homework completed satisfactorily.

Is homework really necessary?

Data from studies in the quite different schools used in the MYW and East Anglian projects clearly demonstrate that, as it stands at present, many pupils do not appear to understand the rationale for homework. In some contexts, the purposes of homework were assumed rather than explicitly explored and developed with pupils. Some pupils saw the value of homework as giving them opportunities to consolidate classwork and to develop their own skills and discipline; others took a longer-term view: 'I reckon we should [get homework] because it's for our own good. Sort of like puts us in a better position to get a better job' (W,Y8,M)[1]. Sometimes pupils acknowledged that they learned more through homework by working in a quieter and more ordered environment:'You'll take it in at home because like you can do it in silence and at school there's always someone talking' (W,Y8,M).

But for every pupil who acknowledged the value of homework in this way, there were many who challenged the whole notion. One pupil (W,Y8,M) even argued that teachers set homework 'just to annoy you'; another commented: 'We don't ask to come to school but we have to and then they give us homework to do in our own time. I don't really think it's fair' (W,Y8,F). Several pupils in both projects felt that enough work was done in school, and that they should not be expected to work at home as well:

> I don't think we need to have homework. I don't think we should get it. We do enough work, I think, in the lessons and working at school. We do five hours at school, and then, I mean, we've had some days where we've had four subjects homework. (E,Y11,M)

In the East Anglian school, boys especially were generally negative about homework. Some agreed, grudgingly, that they *should* get it, and that it could be helpful for tests, but they were reluctant to put much effort into it. Pupils particularly resented homework when lesson time itself did not appear to be used constructively:

> Like when a teacher sets out a lesson and if they don't finish it in time you get that plus the homework they had for you anyway, which isn't really your fault, 'cause the lesson hasn't gone the way they wanted it to, but you're just getting lumbered with extra homework. (E,Y10,M)

---

[1]Quotations from student interviews are referenced as follows: E = East Anglia study; W = Making Your Way study; Y 11, 10 etc. refers to the student's year group; M = male student; F = female student.

Motivation to complete homework was thus low amongst many pupils, and homework was seen as an intrusion rather than an integral part of the educative process.

Maintaining the homework schedule

Another overriding theme to emerge from interviews with school pupils is the need for schools to plan homework demands effectively and coherently across subject departments. Homework timetables and homework diaries existed, but there were frequent complaints that teachers did not abide by the timetable. Pupils' complaints suggested that, if the agreed homework schedule was not strictly adhered to, there were inevitably time-management problems for even the most conscientious pupils, and this could lead to poor quality work, to neglected tasks and to frustration:

> She's supposed to give it us Monday for Thursday, then Friday for Monday. But she gives it us the days like we have a lesson that day and then a lesson the next day, she gives it again so we only have the night to do it. (W,Y10,F)

> It's just that they seem to like, get together and say, oh we're going to give them all homework this week, and you all get it that week. Then the next week you'll hardly have any or just one bit or something. There's supposed to be a homework timetable but it doesn't seem to work. If they stuck to the homework timetable it would be a lot easier to keep it all sort of on an even keel. (E,Y10,F)

These unplanned demands were compounded by the apparent lack of co-ordination between staff. Many teachers, it appeared, expected pupils to give *their* subject priority without taking other commitments into account:

> What really annoys me is that each teacher expects you to take priority in their homework and you get told off if you haven't done it. But you are trying to explain to them that you have got seven other teachers who want you to be able to do this and to take priority over different lessons. (W,Y9,F)

> Every teacher seems to say theirs is the most important, and that it won't take you long, but it *will* take you a long time when you've got all the teachers saying that – they don't realise. (E,Y11,M)

From the teachers' perspective the pressures are understandable. Teachers, after all, are increasingly aware of their school's position in the local league tables. They work in a political context, accountable to governors, headteachers, parents and the pupils themselves. Many may believe that pupils work better in a highly structured environment, and that pupil motivation will falter if pressure is removed. There is undoubtedly some validity in such a view, but equally there are dangers – of resentment and of disengagement.

The difficulties may be exacerbated by the demands of GCSE coursework in years 10 and 11. Many of the East Anglian pupils complained that the uneven demands of homework, and the inflexibility of the homework timetable, meant that there was no opportunity to develop a systematic programme for their coursework submissions, or to revise for 'mock' examinations. The additional demands of coursework and of revision made homework seem an extra burden to be coped with. This lack of co-ordination made the completion of coursework difficult because teachers in other subjects kept setting homework even as deadlines approached. It was clear that pupils wanted their teachers to appreciate their overall workload, to respect them and to acknowledge the fact that there were times when one subject might have to take priority over others.

The pupils' views are quite clear, and show remarkable consistency; their teachers need to plan together more coherently – 'Does *anyone* know all we are expected to do on any one night in year 11?' (E,Y11,F) – and they have to set homework tasks which are realistic with regard to the time they will take and the date on which they are to be submitted. Teachers also need to be seen to acknowledge competing demands from coursework, examination revision, other subjects, and extra-curricular activities. All these appear to be essential ingredients if the potential of homework is to be maximised, and if work done at home is to make a positive contribution to the teaching–learning process.

The importance of homework

Besides problems of co-ordination across subjects, many pupils highlighted problems with the nature of homework itself. Tasks were sometimes unrealistic, with pupils told to finish work off at home, but without access to the necessary resources:

> I think it's 'The Inspector Calls'; it's not very good because we haven't got enough books to go round the class and we've got to share, and it's sometimes one between three...We've got to do homework but can't take a book home so you can't make quotes about the play and it's quite difficult. (W,Y10,M)

At other times, homework seemed merely pointless and rather dull: 'Just finish this off for homework'.

The impression given is that homework does not matter very much: pupils talked of some teachers who often did not bother whether homework was done or not; some failed to set it, particularly in years 8 and 9 ('I've only had two homework's from art this year', W,Y9,M); others attempted to collect it in but made no attempt to remonstrate with those pupils who had not submitted it. Some pupils were apparently told to revise for tests which did not take place, or were set work by teachers who never again made reference to it. In such contexts, there was clearly no incentive for pupils to complete the homework set. Thus, several pupils said things like:

> He doesn't really pay much attention to you. You can just say 'I didn't do it' and he'll just walk off and go and get someone else's. Most of the time it's about five people who hand in their homework. I've stopped handing it in now. (W,Y8,M)

> They don't really bother; they think, oh it's up to you, do it if you want, you know. They give you detentions, but then you don't turn up to them, so it doesn't matter. Normally threats aren't carried out if you don't do your homework. (E,Y11,F)

There was a feeling, too, that homework was unimportant because teachers repeated much of the work in class: 'You have done it in class and when you go home it is just to do the same thing and you already know it' (W,Y9,M). Sometimes pupils claimed that their teachers just thought up something to occupy them, rather than to extend or promote independent study as a valuable exercise. There was a persistent sense that the teachers were wasting the pupils' time: 'They always tell you "don't waste my time" in the lesson, but you think, you're wasting my time giving me this homework' (E,Y11,F).

These views were exacerbated, of course, when the subject was seen to be unattractive or the homework task inaccessible. Thus homework in modern languages was frequently ignored or rushed through during registration, for a variety of reasons: it was seen as too difficult, or lacking utility, or because it was claimed that there were no textbooks to help. Across the ability range, boys especially, but also girls, tended to give very low priority to languages homework, claiming that they could learn enough in the week before the examination! In contrast, and not surprisingly, the most enjoyable subjects and the easiest subjects were usually done first. The East Anglian study reflected gender differences towards subjects in the way in which homework was prioritised. Boys in particular reported that they did the ones they wouldn't get stuck on, which they could do without thinking about: 'like maths, because you've got a question and you answer it. But like English, you have a question and you have to think about the way you'll answer it' (E,Y11,M). Girls, however, often had different priorities: 'If there's an English essay I usually do that first. All the subjects I prefer, and then physics and maths, they get done if I have time' (E,Y10,F).

The nature of the homework task, the status of the subject, the resources available to support the homework task, and the perceived value of the task by the teacher, all profoundly influenced the pupils' reactions to the homework. But pupil reaction was not always negative. Pupils were more inclined to respond positively to homework tasks which allowed for individual initiative or research:

It's like all research now like so it's all right...it's like we're doing a topic on toys...we're doing like make a toy for a young one, an educational one. And for the other DT group, we like [are making] a football kit. And we [are] just asking questionnaires, like questioning the public what they think about football kit, favourite colour and all that. That's all right. (W,Y10,M)

Pupils were equally positive where there appeared to be a clear purpose, such as researching new materials or exploring new issues. In such cases, many pupils appeared willing to research in local libraries or through resources in the home: 'My grandma helps me in history homework because she went for World War One, my great grandma' (W,Y9,M). In such cases, the autonomy, the independence, the sense of discovery, all came together to increase motivation and involvement, to give a renewed zest for learning; then pupils reacted with enthusiasm, commitment and determination: 'Yeah. They gave you lots of time to research. Nobody was interfering with you or giving you set patterns, you could do what you want as long as you achieved the goal' (W,Y9,F). Contrary to expectations, pupils of both sexes said that they enjoyed coursework, which enabled them to research in their own time.

The pupils interviewed thus perceived homework as valuable and important when it was clearly structured into the teaching–learning process, and when it was integrated into the context of a lesson or series of lessons. It may be that a new task was set, or independent research encouraged, or that the homework consolidated and extended the activities of the lesson. Pupils also appreciated it when members of staff set realistic and clearly defined tasks, collected the work in on the appointed day, and dutifully marked and returned the work, appropriately annotated with encouraging and supportive comments, within a reasonable span of time. Such an approach was likely to make sense and to be acknowledged by them as worthwhile.

Conflicting demands

Even when there was a clear point to the work set, however, pupils did not always find it easy to fit in all the homework they were expected to do once GCSE courses were under way in years 10 and 11. One of the main difficulties many pupils faced as they progressed through secondary school (as the MYW data show) was that of reconciling homework with other activities and commitments, and finding the time to fit in all that was required of them. Among activities conflicting with homework were domestic tasks. One boy, for example, claimed: 'You've got your mum and dad saying, "You're getting older now, you can do more stuff", so I have to make my own dinner, have to do the washing up' (E,Y11,M). A Y10 pupil, who lived with her father, said that she rarely had time to do homework because of the burden of domestic responsibilities:

> When I get home I do the washing, I load the washing machine, unload the washing machine, cook the dinner, sit down ten minutes on my homework. Then it's dinner out of the oven, serve it up. My dad comes in from work and that's it. It's gone – it's just housework – it's all I do. (E,Y10,F)

Other pupils in years 10 and 11 said they had weekend jobs, which reduced the time available for homework. Neither domestic nor productive work, however, was frequently mentioned; more often pupils, particularly the boys, said that they had 'better things to do', and that they would rather go out than stay in and do homework. Homework sat in the way of other things, impinging on time which they felt should be their own (see also chapter 10).

Television was often cited as something which interfered with homework time. As one year 11 girl said:

> The television is a very big distraction, I think. You can sit there and write just one line, and then you'll watch a whole programme. Then you'll realise, you'll look at your watch and think, oh I've got to go out now. Pack it up, put it away – and you've done one line. That's what I usually get. That's why I have to go in my room and do it; otherwise I never get it done. (E,Y11,F)

Some pupils did their homework while watching television, but even when pupils went to their own rooms, listening to music or reading might distract them, although some said that listening to music helped concentration.

Several pupils also reflected ironically on a situation where the school was encouraging them to develop extra-curricular activities, in guiding, in an orchestra or a football team, in community work or the local church, or to develop skills such as playing the piano, acting or swimming, while at the same time denying them, because of homework, the time needed to carry out such activities regularly and with commitment: 'They [the teachers] complain if you haven't got a social life...They say "Why don't you get out?" You say "How can I when I have got three hours homework every night?"' (W,Y9,F).

For the conscientious pupil the demands of homework could become almost intolerable:

> You get *too much*...You're at school, and then you get homework, and you stay up ages and you've got no time for yourself. Then you moan about having so much homework, and then your family starts moaning at you...And you start getting behind, and then the teachers give you detentions' cause you ain't done it. (E,Y10,M)

In such a situation, it was not surprising that some opted out of the homework process altogether. This was particularly likely to happen among boys, and among those of both sexes who did not expect to perform very well in their GCSE examinations. Many of the East Anglian boys claimed to spend as short a time as possible on their homework, leaving it to the last minute, not getting work in on time and only doing properly the work they found enjoyable. High achieving girls, on the other hand, tended to spend a long time on homework, especially for subjects like English and History. As one explained, 'Generally it's the girls who will get their homework done, and they won't lose it, or let the dog eat it, or get it wiped off the computer' (E,Y11,F). Girls who did not expect to perform well at GCSE were, however, less committed to completing homework tasks, saying that they tended to put off doing their work as long as they could, although they were still more likely than the boys to complete the work and hand it in.

These gender differences echoed comments made by Harris et al. (1993), and were supported by data from the questionnaires that were used with years 10 and 11 pupils and year 10 parents. The responses showed that 42% of boys, but only 23% of girls, agreed or strongly agreed with the statement that they would rather go out than stay in and do their homework. In the middle schools, only 4 out of 36 girls (11%) but 13 out of 35 boys (37%) agreed or strongly agreed with the statement that they often went out rather than stayed in and did their homework. Thus, there was already a difference in the early stages of secondary schooling in the attitude of boys and girls towards the time they were willing to spend on homework.

These findings were confirmed by the parental responses, which showed a clear gender difference in the amount of time spent on homework by boys and girls. 89% of parents of year 10 girls said that their daughters had an excellent or quite good attitude towards homework, spending at least an hour a night on it, and often more. Comments were made such as: 'She spends a considerable amount of time – more than is necessary sometimes to achieve the standard she has set herself', and 'No time limit is set – she spends as long a time as is needed – up to three hours if necessary. She is conscientious and always does her homework'. Fewer boys, according to parents, were said to have an excellent or quite good attitude towards homework. When asked to comment on boys' attitudes, typical responses were: 'To complete it and get it out of the way as quickly as possible. Done slackly unless leant upon'; and 'Cavalier – rarely seems to do much homework – most of it done at school – feels it's a real imposition on spare time unless it's something he's really interested in'. Several parents of boys said that all homework was completed, but that the boys would spend no longer than necessary. Parents with children of both sexes (75 parents representing 58 families in total) were asked whether there were any differences in attitudes to learning which they had observed in their sons and daughters. 44 parents thought there was a difference, with 31 suggesting that their daughters were more hard-working, took their work more seriously and were generally more conscientious, while their sons left everything until the last minute, were less mature than girls of a similar age and were less interested in school work.

The school–home partnership

Several researchers (for example, Leone and Richards, 1989; Miller and Kelley, 1991; Olympia et al., 1994) highlight the importance of parental involvement in the homework process, and it seems clear that the full potential of homework will only be realised, and the high expectations of school management teams fulfilled, when schools take effective steps to involve parents and to ensure they understand the nature and role of homework. At a basic level, this can be achieved most easily if parents check that homework tasks have been completed, and confirm this by signing pupils' homework diaries. This may seem an extremely simple requirement in the school–home partnership, yet the data suggest that most parents checked their children's homework only occasionally. Perhaps because they recognised the more laid-back attitude of their sons, parents were more likely to check boys' homework frequently. In addition, parents who expected their children to get seven or more A-C grades at GCSE were more likely to check their homework frequently than, ironically, those expecting their children to get fewer higher grades.

The pupil interviews confirmed that parental involvement was often limited or ineffectual: 'Yes, she wants me to stay in until I have done it. So if I have to go somewhere I tell her I haven't got none' (W,Y9,M) and: 'They tend to just leave it to me, and so they're not bothered about what homework I'm doing or not, so on most occasions I'm not getting the homework in on time at all' (E,Y10,M). On occasions, though, there was evidence that various forms of incentive or threat were effective in focusing the minds of the pupils: 'Yes, every night it's "Have you got homework to do – then do it". There's no way in the world I'd get away with not doing homework with my parents' (E,Y10,M). And then there is the battle with the 'soaps':

> Well I have my tea, and mum says, 'If you don't get your homework done you are *not* watching *Home and Away* and *Neighbours.'* And I do it straight away. I have *got* to watch *Home and Away* and *Neighbours*. (W,Y9,F)

Ideally, however, the home ought not simply to have a passive role, linked to mothers – who were invariably mentioned by pupils in this role – monitoring the homework set. School Staff Handbooks frequently stress the value of the home in offering encouragement, support and advice to pupils, and project images of parents discussing homework tasks with pupils and helping to resolve uncertainties and difficulties. This may be an image of perfection and an unrealistic expectation in some contexts, because of differing role models, socio-economic constraints and pressures of time. But some pupils did experience such support, although interestingly, it was invariably fathers who were quoted in this context: 'My dad helps me a lot with my maths, and that's because he was good at maths, and he wants me to have a very good job when I'm older' (W,Y8,F) and: 'I live with my dad, and he's really good because there's only me and him in the house...he'll help me with science if I don't get it' (E,Y10,F). Such comments were rare, however – the exception rather than the rule – and it appeared more likely that parents felt unable, because of lack of ability or time, to participate as much as they might in the extension of their children's learning through homework: 'My mum takes some interest in it, but she's very busy, and my dad's away quite a bit, so I usually get on on my own' (E,Y10,M).

The 'triumph of hope over experience'?

This chapter has focused on pupils' perceptions of homework. In certain contexts and under certain conditions, some pupil voices clearly show that homework can be an enjoyable and valuable experience, extending and consolidating learning, promoting independent learning and research skills, developing perseverance and self-discipline, and enhancing the quality of the teaching–learning process. Little of this will surprise many teachers: it is part of their own justification for homework and it is explicitly stated in many staff handbooks.

However, a quite different and much more negative pupil view was so widespread – boys and girls, in different areas, schools, years and classes – that it cannot easily be dismissed. Many pupils gave us the impression that the volume of homework, the general dullness and lack of interest of many of the tasks set, and the competing demands from other subjects and other activities, means that they are overwhelmed and simply cannot cope, especially in years 10 and 11. In some cases, the result is that no homework is completed: the pupils are simply worn down by the competing pressures and stresses. The boredom and frustration expressed in comments made by some pupils surely cannot support and enrich learning. They lead us to suggest that schools need to re-evaluate their approaches to homework, and to consider exactly what is essential. The pupil voices suggest that a number of explicit questions ought to be addressed:

- Is the rationale for homework clearly explained and understood by pupils, teachers and parents?
- Is the homework timetable effectively and fairly implemented by all staff for all pupils?
- Is the time requirement for homework realistic, and can the tasks be completed by most pupils in the designated time?
- Is the nature of the homework stimulating and interesting, and does it involve different approaches and types of activity?
- Are homework tasks sometimes differentiated according to pupil ability and need?
- Is feedback to pupils regular, appropriate and supportive?
- How often is homework a legitimate concern for a staff development programme, to ensure consistency within and between departments?
- How much of the homework set for any pupil in any subject over any term is really worthwhile, and positively supports the teaching–learning process?

Schools explicitly and openly addressing these questions may well be closer to fulfilling the potential of homework and enriching the teaching–learning process for all those involved. At the same time, there is a need to recognise young people's legitimate concerns about having some time for themselves in which to pursue their own personal and social agenda. Only then, perhaps, will schools' approaches to the homework problem represent the triumph of experience over hope.

References

Cooper, H. (1994) *The Battle Over Homework*. Thousand Oaks, California: Corwin

Press, Inc.

Cowie, H. and Rudduck, J. (1990) *Learning Together – Working Together, Vol.3*. London, BP International Ltd.

Department of Education and Science (1987) *Education Observed 4 – Homework – A Report by HM Inspectors*. London: HMSO.

Harris, S., Nixon, J. and Rudduck, J. (1993) 'School work, homework and gender'. *Gender and Education*, **5**, 1, 3–15.

Harris, S. and Rudduck, J. (1993) 'Establishing the seriousness of learning in the early years of secondary schooling'. *British Journal of Educational Psychology*, **63**, 322–336.

Holmes, M. and Croll, P. (1989) 'Time spent on homework and academic achievement'. *Educational Research*, **31**, 1, 36–45.

Keith, T. (1982) 'Time spent on homework and high school grades: a large-sample path analysis'. *Journal of Educational Psychology*, **74**, 248–253.

Keith, T. and Page, E. (1985) 'Homework works at school: national evidence for policy changes'. *School Psychology Review*, **14**, 351–359.

Keith, T., Reimers, T., Fehrman, P., Potter-Baum, S. and Aubey, L. (1986) 'Parental involvement, homework and TV time: direct and indirect effects on high school achievement. *Journal of Educational Psychology*, **78**, 5, 373-380.

Keith, T. and Cool, V. (1992) 'Testing models of school learning: effects of quality of instruction, motivation, academic coursework, and homework on academic achievement'. *School Psychology Quarterly*, **7**, 3, 207–226.

Leone, C. and Richards, M. (1989) 'Classwork and homework in early adolescence: the ecology of achievement'. *Journal of Youth and Adolescence*, **18**, 6, 531–548.

MacBeath, J. and Turner, M. (1990) *Learning Out of School: Homework, Policy and Practice*. Glasgow: Jordanhill College.

Miller, D. and Kelley, M. (1991) 'Interventions for improving homework performance: a critical review'. *School Psychology Quarterly*, **63**, 174–185.

Natriello, G. and McDill, E. (1986) 'Performance Standards, Student Effort on Homework and Academic Achievement'. *Sociology of Education*, **59**, 18–31.

Olympia, D., Sheridan, S. and Jenson, W. (1994) 'Homework: a natural means of home–school collaboration'. *School Psychology Quarterly*, **9**, 1, 60–80.

Paschal, R., Weinstein, T. and Walberg, H. (1984) 'The effects of homework on learning: a quantitative synthesis'. *Journal of Educational Research*, **78**, 2, 97–104.

Rutter, M., Maughan, B., Mortimore, P. and Ouston, J. (1979) *15,000 Hours*. London: Open Books.

Walberg, H. et al. (1985) 'Homework's Powerful Effects on Learning'. *Educational Leadership*, **42**, 7, 76–79.

Wootton, M. (1992) *Homework*. Upminster: Nightingale Teaching Consultancy.

CHAPTER 8

Making a strategic withdrawal: disengagement and self-worth protection in male pupils

Roland Chaplain

Teachers get on my nerves. When I do a good piece of work they put a red line through it!

Asked 'Is there any point in working hard in school?' one pupil (Y9,M) gave the above response. The pupil was perceived by his form teacher as having a 'low level of motivation' towards school work. From the pupil's perspective whatever he did was not valued: when pupils believe that teachers do not value their work it tends to lower their self-concept; the pupil quoted above scored very low on the self-concept scale he completed.

This chapter is concerned with how male pupils perceive their self and social identities. It also looks at teachers' constructs of disengaged male pupils and how they think pupils see themselves. Explaining a pupil's lack of motivation to achieve is not simply related to ability but is influenced by personal and interpersonal processes, as Thompson (1994) points out:

> All too familiar to educators...is the student who consistently underachieves despite an apparent ability to cope with the demands of his or her studies. Such behaviour may cloak a pattern of self-worth protection in student achievement motivation. (p. 259)

The motivation to protect their sense of self-worth results in pupils using a range of tactics to avoid damage to their self-esteem. While such tactics are effective in the short term, 'the enduring consequence is under-achievement' (ibid.). Self-worth protection, or the general tendency to establish and maintain a positive image, draws together the relationship between success (or failure) at school, self-image and social value. Furthermore, Covington (1992) highlights the relationships between ability – that quality highly regarded in education – and feelings of self-esteem and personal worth. He goes on to suggest:

> It is not surprising that the pupil's sense of esteem often becomes equated with ability – to be able is to be valued as a human being but to do poorly is evidence of inability, and reason to despair of one's worth. (p. 16)

There is considerable evidence to illustrate the effects (intended and unintended) of having high and low levels of expectation about the competence of others. Most research into these effects, in school contexts, was inspired by the work of Rosenthal and Jacobson (1968) and there can be few teachers who have trained since that time who are unaware of *Pygmalion in the Classroom*. This book reported the effects of teacher expectations on pupil performance. Although the study was criticised (Elashoff and Snow, 1971), the idea of teachers effecting a 'self-fulfilling prophecy' grabbed the hearts and minds of many interested commentators of the time.

Most research into teacher expectations has been concerned with the *positive* outcomes of the process – looking at the 'Halo' effect: that is, bias that can lead teachers, on the basis of some irrelevant characteristic, to rate some individuals more highly than they actually merit. Research into the *negative* effects of having low expectations, the 'Golem' effect (see Babad et al., 1982), has tended to be studied by simulation rather than naturalistic observation. Interest in the effects of teachers' expectations continues, both among researchers and policy makers (see, for example, Carr and Kurtz-Costes, 1994; Alexander et al., 1992). To illustrate its potential in the development of disengaged, underachieving and anti-school pupils we shall turn to a model produced by Harris and Rosenthal (1986) to help unravel the process. Attention to this model can provide a framework for proactive (rather than reactive) interventions. The model argues that there are three components to the teacher expectancy process:

1. forming impressions
2. communicating our beliefs
3. effects on others.

We form impressions about pupils on the basis of our understanding of how they should behave and are behaving. Such understandings are important in explaining how we categorise and respond to other people. Social psychologists argue that we carry implicit models of people around with us, often unconsciously, that contain stereotypical attributes of personality that we believe others possess. Certain traits are central to forming impressions from which we infer a whole range of other traits or behaviours. These impressions are held about social groups (such as football supporters), types of people (such as introverts), and individuals. Rosenberg et al. (1968) suggested that these models have two key dimensions: mental ability and sociability, and within each dimension we hold 'good' and 'bad' examples. As teachers, we might have a hypothetical model of the 'ideal' pupil: attentive, clean, considerate, respectful, hard working, intelligent. It is against such a model that we measure other children and predict their likely academic or social behaviour. As a teacher, the ability to predict the likely performance ability of a pupil is a salient skill.

The second component of the model is the transmission of these beliefs to pupils, through what we say, how we say it, and the postures and gestures which accompany the language. Particular combinations of these behaviours project either a positive or a negative classroom climate. Harris and Rosenthal (1986) show, for example, that both the *quality* and *quantity* of interactions between teachers and engaged or disengaged pupils differ.

Thirdly, there are the short and long-term outcomes for those involved. The way in which messages from teachers are received and interpreted by pupils affects their motivation, performance, attitude and social behaviour. There is a large body of evidence which shows how pupils develop effective (and ineffective) motivational styles influenced primarily by causes they *attribute* to their past successes and failures (see Weiner, 1992). Those who think their successes are due to their ability and their failures to lack of effort are likely, if repeated over time, to develop effective styles. Conversely, those who think their failures are caused by their lack of ability and put their successes down to luck are likely to develop ineffective styles. Thus, the pattern of explanations individuals develop determines their subsequent willingness to maintain effort – or to give up! Pupils who interpret messages about their performance and behaviour in a negative way are also likely to infer a range of other beliefs about themselves, and teachers, which are likely to lower their self-esteem. In response to uncertainty about their ability, and to maintain positive beliefs about themselves, they may adopt tactics based on other areas of personal strength to persuade others, not necessarily teachers, to hold them in positive regard. Such endeavours might include disengagement from learning tasks by direct action (such as disruption) or by indirect action (such as work avoidance). The type of feedback which teachers provide is considered to be central in influencing the attributions their pupils make about their learning. In this chapter we will examine the data from the *Disengagement and Male Underachievement* study using the three components from Harris and

Rosenthal's (1986) model as a framework in order to determine where in the process educators might intervene.

How we carried out our study

From the data in the *Making Your Way Through Secondary School* study (see chapter 1), we identified a number of individual pupils who, during the course of their school careers, were in danger of becoming disengaged from learning and schooling. We decided, therefore, to look at the issues in more detail in three other comprehensive schools, part of a TVEE Consortium in the North of England, which had all expressed interest in disengagement and underachievement among male pupils.

This research looks at how disengaged pupils perceive themselves: in terms of their competency as learners; in relation to others; and what they perceive as obstructing their engagement with learning. These perceptions are believed to be important in understanding the self-worth motive. In addition we were interested to see if these perceptions were common among all disengaged pupils and if they differed from those of engaged pupils.

In each school we asked teachers to identify a group of male pupils, from years 8 and 9, whom they perceived as disengaged from learning and/or schooling, and others in the same years who were thought to be ⁻ng. ـed. We do not know whether teachers chose pupils who were 'moderately/occasionally disengaged' or 'very/frequently disengaged'; there were certainly references among the disengaged group in each school to 'the others' who were characterised as being more disruptive and more inclined not to attend school than they were. This may in fact be the case, or it may be a device used by the pupils for protecting their self-worth and social identity.

We gathered data from pupils by semi-structured interview in one school and questionnaire (based on the interview schedule) in the other two schools. Some pupils, although in school on the day, opted not to attend for interview and the final numbers across the three schools were 32 disengaged pupils and 2ⁱ engaged pupils. The interviews were conducted in one day with three researchers each interviewing six or seven pupils. The questionnaires were sent directly to the other two schools and distributed by teachers. Anonymity, for those completing questionnaires, was ensured by providing each pupil with an envelope which was returned sealed to their teacher who then returned the whole bundle to the researchers. In addition to the interviews and questionnaires, all three groups of pupils were asked to complete a scale designed to measure their *self-concept as a learner*[1]. The scale consists of 13 items that are positively framed (for example, I am usually eager to go to lessons) and 13 that are negatively framed (for example, I give up easily in school work). We also asked teachers to complete an *inferred self-concept scale*[2] in which they were asked to say how they thought each pupil perceived himself. Teachers were asked to rate each pupil's sense of self-worth, to make judgements about how they related to others, and how they perceived teachers. The object of administering these scales was to ascertain, firstly, if and how engaged and disengaged pupils differ in their feelings about themselves and, secondly, to provide some insight into if and how teachers differentiate between the two groups of pupils.

How we see them: teachers' models of disengaged boys

We invited interested teachers from the school in which we conducted the interviews to send us their thoughts on disengagement. The responses of the 25 who replied were interesting – not the least because of the differences in perception. Some thought that it was a relatively recent phenomenon but teachers of long experience saw it as a familiar problem, mainly affecting adolescent working-class boys. Also interesting was the tendency in the teachers' responses to locate the source of the problem within the pupils themselves, in their family background or in their community. (This tendency for people to 'externalise' responsibility for problems is familiar – see for instance, Totman, 1982; Lawrence and Steed, 1986.) Most of the teachers attributed responsibility to 'within-pupil' factors. These factors were concerned with *anti-social tendencies* (such as behaviour problems); *intellectual capacity* (for example, low ability or lack of effort); with *personality* (for example, low self-esteem); and with *stage of development* (for example, adolescence). Parents were also held responsible in some cases, being perceived as 'uncaring' or 'overprotective'. There was, however, a core of common ground in that a number of teachers built their explanations around the idea of disengaged pupils protecting 'self-esteem' and needing to maintain their 'social identity' within the peer group. They noted that 'maintaining street credibility' required indifference on the part of male pupils to routine requirements. It was not 'cool' for disengaged boys to be seen to be paying serious attention to school work or homework. 'Young men', said one teacher, 'have to be coaxed to work', whereas girls accept the need more readily and without loss of face (see chapter 7). And teachers acknowledged that because most girls were more receptive they tended to get more help in class. But some teachers saw, beneath the tough or nonchalant exteriors, young men who had 'a desperate need for friends, for confirmation'. None recognised a desire in these pupils to succeed academically and only one felt that negative messages from teachers might be a contributing factor. More women than men suggested that the need to maintain the 'macho male stereotype' was a key factor in disengagement.

Teachers said that by year 10 pupils were aware how hard academic work was becoming; the less academically inclined 'realise that school is coming to an end...and this frightens them' – particularly those who still have problems with the basic skills of reading and writing. Aware of their shortcomings in these important areas some become 'insecure and scared'. Clearly, as some teachers pointed out, those with a poor attendance record (whether the result or the cause of disengagement) do not know how to catch up, may 'feel they are failing' and disengage as a way of masking their fear of failure; in short, they avoid the situation which is the source of failure. However, there is evidence to show that teachers' perceptions of children's abilities, self-concepts and motivations are too general and heavily biased by academic achievement levels (see Carr and Kurtz-Costes, 1994).

Getting the message across: teacher–pupil communication and disengagement

Harris and Rosenthal (1986) argued that in order for teachers' beliefs about high and low-ability pupils to have an effect on achievement and behaviour, they need to be transmitted (verbally and non-verbally) and be *accepted* by the pupils. Children can, it appears, accurately detect the differences in teacher communication to high and low achievers from a very early age (see, for instance, Babad et al., 1991). In this section we take up this theme which seems, from our data, to be a pivotal factor in pupils' attitudes towards school and learning and in their sense of identity and self-worth.

Adolescent pupils have a very strong sense of justice and the disengaged pupils were particularly ready to write or talk about incidents where they thought that they had been treated unfairly. Teachers 'not being fair' usually meant getting the blame for something you hadn't done or being suspected of bad behaviour just because you'd behaved badly in the past. A disengaged pupil commented:

> There are some [teachers] who like everyone else and they take it out on me. Well, everyone will be talking in class and if I am talking then they'll take it out on me and no one else...Just one of those things...they get on to me and no one else.

Some pupils felt that it was so difficult to change the image that the teachers had of them that there was little point in trying to reform and settle down to work. Not surprisingly, while two thirds of the engaged pupils thought teachers were fair to them, two thirds of disengaged pupils thought teachers were *not* fair to them. The more engaged pupils acknowledged that teachers sometimes picked on pupils with a reputation based on past misbehaviour: 'It's like if you've done anything in the past wrong they keep you in mind, and anything done, they'll blame you'. Another engaged pupil commented: 'I noticed people being victimised'; and a third mentioned a pupil who used to get into a lot of trouble when he came to the school (he'd changed schools several times) and even though now 'he's calmed down like, Mr [teacher] just picks on him'. Engaged pupils were also upset by 'unfair' treatment being 'dished out' to them; they felt aggrieved, for instance, about being bracketed with disruptive pupils and punished *en masse* for what only one or two had done.

The disengaged pupils were also sensitive to what they saw as teachers neglecting their interests in favour of the girls. Indeed, one pupil said quite explicitly that he had lost interest in school work when he saw that teachers were giving girls more help than he received. There are several comments, from different pupils, on this theme:

> Some of them [teachers] seem to edge towards the girls I would say...They're sort of kinder to girls. If there's a small job to be done...or a special job to be done, usually it's the girls who get it.

> A few of them [teachers] are sexist. It's all, like, some blokes favour the lads, some blokes favour the girls.

> They're not very fair to anyone except the girls.

The disengaged pupils were clear in expressing their dislike of being humiliated by teachers in front of their peers. One pupil commented on teachers who deliberately picked on pupils whom they expected not to know the answers and made them look stupid in front of the class. They also felt that teachers took no notice of what they were trying to say – in short, they disliked teachers who did not take them seriously, even though *they* acknowledged that they had not always taken learning seriously. Pupils of this age (13 to 14) don't like to be treated as 'inferior'; they don't like it if teachers 'try to make you look small'; they don't like being judged 'by what your appearance is like'. As we can see, a lot of these comments are to do with image and with sense of self.

Behind the 'I'm not bothered' front adopted, like a bullet-proof vest, as a form of self-worth protection were many pupils who said, in a one-to-one interview (or in response to a questionnaire) that they would really like to do well in school and receive the support of their teachers, not only with their work but also with sorting out some aspects of their social lives. The 'authenticity' of the teacher was, not surprisingly, seen as important by both engaged and disengaged pupils. Pupils chose to talk to teachers whom they felt would understand them, who were likely to listen, who might be ready to share a joke, who wouldn't let them down and whose own style was not too distant from that of the pupils. A disengaged pupil explained why he talked about things with a teacher he liked and trusted: 'He understands what you feel. I think it's because all the things you've done, he's already done when he was younger.' Another disengaged pupil talked about his form tutor, whom he felt comfortable with:

> I've been with her three years and I know her like dead well. When we have PSE and Circle Time and that's really good...she's relaxed about it; she gets mad when she wants to but she's usually...Like...I'm late for registration when we've been playing football at dinner and so she'll let that go, and if I'm late three times, she'll ask me if something is wrong at home and that. She'll keep close to everyone and there's quite a few people in the class whose mums and dads have split up during the three years and she's always helped them.

On the other hand, some disengaged pupils felt that they couldn't talk to teachers about things that worried them because they would be embarrassed or because they felt that their trust might be betrayed. Some pupils were put off seeking help from teachers because such a move did not fit their nonchalant image: 'It's OK for girls, not for boys' and 'Not me, because I'm not that sort of...I don't like getting involved with teachers, you know...anything personal like that. It's just me'. And if pupils did want to talk things through with their teachers they preferred privacy: 'A tutor is the last person you tell, because you have to say it in front of everybody else in your group and considering this is the person you are supposed to tell...There is no one else'.

It seems that the presence of teachers who are prepared to listen, who are understanding, who are approachable, who are fair, and who do not seek to humiliate pupils is a crucially important aspect of school life. And while engaged pupils are as ready as disengaged pupils to comment critically on teachers who are unfair, it is the disengaged pupils who more often, according to their accounts of the situation, claim that they are being treated unfairly and who receive more negative messages from teachers. The consequent loss of self-esteem can also come from situations involving the peer group. A number of disengaged pupils (those who tended to be withdrawn and socially isolated rather than the noisily and 'collaboratively' disengaged) said that they had experienced being bullied and other forms of harassment. One pupil said that he had been called 'fat bastard'; another recalled a very painful period: 'Everyone used to call me queer and gay and everything, all of the time...I just tried to ignore them but they just took all my friends off me...'. Clothes and possessions seemed to feature quite a lot in the incidents of harassment – what one pupil referred to as 'snob stuff'. Pupils said that name-calling and bullying were reasons why pupils in their year group were fed up with school and confirmed that the major targets for this kind of abuse were 'people who aren't very well off'. What is at stake here is how pupils feel about themselves. One said, 'Nobody likes me'; another referred to 'stupid people who don't like me even if they don't know me'. It is not easy for pupils to seek help from teachers in these circumstances without risking further loss of self-esteem.

Across the three schools, both engaged and disengaged pupils thought that they should be treated in a more adult fashion, or with more respect, once they were teenagers. More of the engaged pupils suggested that reciprocity was the right thing to aim for: 'If we behaved better then teachers would treat us with more respect', or, from a slightly different angle, 'If we were treated more like adults we'd behave more like adults'; and, again, 'Yes, we are getting older and more mature so if they treat us with more respect we would probably treat them with respect'.

The picture that the pupils draw suggests that they are aware of their difficulties – a picture, consistent with the self-concept scale results, which shows that disengaged pupils tend to have a poor self-image in relation to academic work. The pupils also show a learned distrust of teachers in general (although they are positive about the qualities of those teachers whom they do respect). While the overall degree of alienation may not be extreme, there is clearly a problem as to how teachers can intervene to help and support pupils who have constructed the situation as one in which teachers, and not the pupils themselves, are a major source of their difficulty with school work.

Examining the effects: how engaged and disengaged pupils see themselves and how teachers think pupils see themselves

The third component of the model – the effects – are discussed in this section. Given the relationship between self-concept and achievement we elected to compare the self-concepts of engaged and disengaged pupils. Although the data suggested that both engaged and disengaged pupils wanted, in the main, to do well at school, overall there were differences[3] between the two groups in the way they perceived themselves as learners and in the way they tackled their school work. Central to the motive to protect self-worth is the relationship between wanting to do well in order to be perceived in a positive light, uncertainty about how and if this can be achieved, and the dynamics of failure-avoiding behaviour. A comparison of scores from the pupil completed *self-concept as a learner scale* for the engaged and disengaged pupils showed that the scores of the disengaged pupils were significantly lower on every aspect of the scale. The disengaged pupils felt that they had greater difficulty in particular with *task orientation* and with more abstract *problem solving* tasks. They were more likely to experience difficulties with writing, coping with tests and doing homework. They were less likely to feel good about their school work. The disengaged pupils also indicated that they had a tendency to give up more easily in school work, to do things without thinking, to make mistakes because they didn't listen, and to give up if they didn't understand something. The responses to the *inferred self-concept scale* (completed by teachers) indicated that they believed disengaged pupils had more negative perceptions of themselves, of themselves in relation to others, and of teachers.

Comparing the overall results from year 8 and year 9, pupils' ratings of themselves were not statistically significant (and we therefore treated them as one group). However, engaged pupils in year 9 tended to score higher than those in year 8. It would appear that their positive self-images improve as they grow older. In contrast, pupils who had low perceptions of themselves (disengaged) in year 8 are likely to find those negative feelings strengthened by the time they reach the end of year 9. (Here we are, of course, extrapolating data from two separate year groups and not looking at the same pupils over time.) This suggests that as pupils move towards the end of their school careers the differences between the engaged and disengaged groups are likely to become more marked. This result is mirrored, but more strongly, in the scale completed by teachers. As the more motivated groups improve their academic performance, their self-concept, so teachers think, is likely to be enhanced; and as the less well-motivated pupils fall behind, teachers believe that their self-image becomes increasingly negative.

We can summarise our observations about how disengaged pupils perceive themselves and others – based on the data from the self-completion scales, from the interviews and from the questionnaires – in the following way:

1. *Perceptions of themselves*
   disengaged pupils:
   - have lower self-concepts and self-esteem than engaged peers;
   - have characteristics that tend to make it difficult to achieve academically; these include: 'giving up easily at school work', 'impulsiveness', 'difficulties in understanding their work', being embarrassed if asked questions publicly or singled out for special attention;
   - are more likely to be fed up with school on a regular basis.

2. *Perceptions of school work*
   disengaged pupils:
   - find homework difficult, given they are often already struggling in class;
   - dislike subjects with a high proportion of writing (e.g. English);
   - dislike subjects where they do not understand (esp. modern languages);
   - have increased anxiety about their ability, as they near exams, because of earlier poor performances.

3. *Relationship with peers*
   disengaged pupils:
   - are more likely to have been involved in bullying incidents;
   - feel under pressure from their immediate friends if they exhibit achievement behaviour;
   - are perceived by many of their engaged peers as a hindrance and annoyance to their own classroom work.

4. *Relationship with teachers*
   disengaged pupils:
   - perceive teachers as generally unfair to *pupils*, but particularly unfair to them;
   - believe that teachers express negative behaviours towards them both verbally and non-verbally;
   - would like a teacher they could trust to talk things through with;
   - consider teachers to be largely responsible for their failure at school.

5. *Perceptions of the future*
   disengaged pupils:
   - show high levels of anxiety about their future chances in the working world;
   - despite negative messages from school want to persist and have some examination success;
   - see a direct relationship between examination success and getting a job;
   - are more likely to plan to get a job at 16.

What can be done to make things better?

We asked all the pupils involved in the study how they felt schools could be improved for those who were 'fed up' or who were disengaged. Both engaged and disengaged pupils were constructive in their suggestions. They said that school work needed to be made more interesting, that pupils should be given more opportunities to find things out for themselves, that classes needed to be smaller 'so the teacher will be able to get round better and help more people'. Some pupils asked for more active learning, 'with more group work and things'. Pupils said that teachers needed to learn to listen to pupils and needed to explain things more. Some pupils thought it would help if there were more choice – more opportunities for them to exercise control over content or pace of work. And some – mainly those who were not so engaged with more academic study – made suggestions that reflected their ambivalence towards school work. They attended school but they wanted more, and longer, breaks between lessons; another proposed a ten o'clock start and one suggested putting an extra hour on each day so that everyone could have Friday off! On a more realistic note, one pupil thought the timetables should be adapted 'so that each day had something to lighten the mood'. Another thought that it should be compulsory to attend 'the important lessons, like maths, history and English, so that they still get some education', but that outside the core curriculum pupils should choose what they wanted to work hard at.

There were several recommendations that referred to the behaviour of teachers, including, predictably, teachers being fairer to pupils, teachers respecting you more, less continuous teacher talk, teachers being a bit more friendly, teachers joking a bit more and teachers giving positive and supportive attention to 'us boys more often'. Pupils put off by lessons which involved a lot of writing (and there were a number who mentioned this) wanted more alternatives for 'people who don't enjoy writing or drawing'. Pupils who were not making good progress with their learning wanted more support teachers who could spend more time with them. Some pupils wanted 'less stressful exams and tests [that] put pressure on [us]'. They also wanted better measures to deal with bullying and name-calling. One pupil suggested bringing together all the pupils who were not motivated and 'ask them what they want to be changed. Yeah, what they want. Then tell them what they *could* have...and find out what they would like out of those options'.

There were a couple of pupils who believed things could not be changed: one said 'School's run how school's run'; he went on: 'School shouldn't fit in for individuals; individuals should fit in with school...so if they choose not to stick with school, it's them isn't it, it's not me. So I'm not worried about them'. This was perhaps a less generous comment than those made by many of the pupils who responded to our questions. Another pupil defended the school's approach saying, 'It's not the school. The school does their best to help them, talk to them. If they are in trouble they put them on report and they do well while they're on report. It's just that they stop once they're off'. Here there was a sense of the higher-attaining pupils beginning to distance themselves from groups or individuals in their year who were stopping them working or getting them in trouble – another possible blow to the self-esteem of the pupils who were most at risk.

In this chapter we have examined the data from three perspectives: teachers' implicit models of the disengaged; disengaged boys' explanations and interpretations of how teachers relate to them; and the effect that 'messages' from teachers have on pupils' sense of self-worth as learners and on their social identities.

The starting point for improvement concerns teachers. Being proactive in preventing the development of negative cycles calls for teachers to appraise their implicit models of disengaged pupils. This would require them to examine their causal explanations of pupils' behaviour and reflect on the messages that they are communicating to pupils. Thompson (1994) reminds us of the importance of teachers in this process:

> Whilst it might be assumed teachers are in a prime position to actively shape their pupils' perceptions of their successes and failures, there is evidence that this potential is either largely unexploited or (more seriously) distorted in its application. (p. 266)

The second point concerns changing the ways in which vulnerable pupils think about their successes and failures. Perceptions of ability are central to the argument. Ability is a highly-valued asset in education and is perceived as a stable characteristic. Being seen to have ability is usually associated with having a positive self-image. Pupils, unsure of their ability and trying to protect their self-image, often conclude it is better not to bother trying rather than to try and fail. If pupils make a real effort to succeed which ends in failure, this can lead to feelings of shame and lower their self-perception.

To help pupils overcome these difficulties and develop a more effective motivational style requires intervention at two levels. The first is the need to teach and encourage these pupils to think differently about the reasons for their successes and failures – to reconsider their understanding of the relationship between ability and effort. The second relates to classroom organisation or, more specifically, the use of non-competitive learning structures. Effective interventions using these strategies with pupils have been reported (see, for example: Covington, 1984; Craske, 1988; Thompson, 1994).

Comparatively little attention has been given to looking at how pupils' explanations and advice might be utilised to improve their learning in schools – but some of the messages are clear. They are about relationships and respect – what Hargreaves (1982) called the 'dignity' of young people. Indeed, the present study has some grounds for optimism. Not only does it offer an agenda that can be acted on; it also suggests that, despite having difficulties in adjusting to the culture of schooling, most disengaged pupils still want to work hard. It is to the credit of those pupils who know they are not doing well in school – know there are things they don't understand, know they haven't a proper command of the strategies for learning effectively – that so many of them still struggle on in what they often perceive as a difficult and unsupportive environment.

Notes

[1] The measure used was a modified version of the Self-Concept as a Learner Scale (Purkey, 1967). The modifications were to reduce the number of items from 50 to 25, and to anglicise the language (the original version is American). One new item was added (*I am able to influence decisions which affect my school work*) to measure the amount of control students felt they had over their learning: what psychologists call 'locus of control'. 13 items were positively framed (e.g., *I am usually eager to go to lessons*) and 13 were negatively framed (*I give up easily in school work*). The scale was subdivided into four sections: motivation (9 items); task orientation (8 items); problem solving (4 items); class membership (4 items). The overall scale was found to be statistically reliable (Cronbach's α=.85).

[2] This was a modified version of an existing measure: the Inferred Self-Concept Scale (Combs and Soper, 1963). There were 15 items in all, which were broken down into three sections each containing five items. The teacher was asked to rate how he/she thought: the students felt about themselves as individuals (e.g., adequate-inadequate); as they related to others (e.g., unimportant-important); and their perception of teachers (e.g., hindering-helpful). A modification was made to the title of the final section. In the original scale respondents are asked to rate how they consider the student perceives 'others'; in our version they were asked *specifically* about how they consider the student perceives teachers. The overall scale was found to be statistically reliable (Cronbach's α =.95).

[3] All scores between the different groups (engaged–disengaged, year 8–year 9, and schools attended) were compared statistically using analysis of variance. All scores for engaged and disengaged differed and the differences were statistically significant. Differences between year 8 and year 9 scores and between the three schools were not statistically significant. A more detailed account of these findings, including results of the statistical analysis, will be published elsewhere (Chaplain, in preparation).

References

Alexander, R., Rose. J. and Woodhead, C. (1992) *Curriculum Organisation and Classroom Practice in Primary Schools*. London : DES.

Babad, E., Inbar, J. and Rosenthal, R.(1982) 'Pygmalion, Galatea and the Golem: investigations of biased and unbiased teachers'. *Journal of Educational Psychology*, 74, 459–474.

Babad, E., Bernieri, F. and Rosenthal, R. (1991) 'Students as judges of teachers' verbal and non-verbal behaviour'. *American Educational Research Journal*, 28, 211–234.

Carr, M. and Kurtz-Costes, B.E. (1994) 'Is being smart everything? The influence of student achievement on teachers' perceptions'. *British Journal of Educational Psychology*, 64, 263–276.

Chaplain, R., Miles, S. and Rudduck, J. (1994) 'Disengagement and Male Underachievement'. School Profile Study No.4. Cambridge: Homerton Publications.

Chaplain, R. 'Self-concept and disengagement: teacher and pupil perspectives' (in press).

Combs, A.W. and Soper, D.W. (1963) *The Relationship of Child Perceptions to Achievement and behaviour in the early school years*. US Department of Health Cooperative Research Project, No. 814.

Covington, M.V. (1984) 'The motive for self-worth', in R. Ames and C. Ames (eds) *Research on Motivation in Education (Vol. 1)*. New York : Academic Press.

Covington, M.V. (1992) *Making the Grade: A Self-Worth Perspective on Motivation and School Reform*. New York : Cambridge University Press.

Covington, M.V., Spratt, M.F. and Omelich, C.E. (1980) 'Is effort enough or does diligence count too?: Student and teacher reactions to effort stability in failure'. *Journal of Educational Psychology*, 72, 446–459.

Craske, M. L. (1988) 'Learned helplessness, self worth motivation and attribution retraining for primary school children'. *British Journal of Educational Psychology*, 58, 152–64.

Elashoff, J.D. and Snow, R.E. (eds) (1971) *Pygmalion Reconsidered*. Washington: Charles A. Jones.

Hargreaves, D.H. (1982) *The Challenge for the Comprehensive School*. London: Routledge and Kegan Paul.

Harris, M.J. and Rosenthal, R. (1986) 'Four factors in the mediation of teacher expectancy effects', in R.S.Feldman (ed.) *The Social Psychology of Education: Current Research and Theory*. New York : Cambridge University Press.

Lawrence, J. and Steed, D. (1986) 'Primary school perceptions of disruptive behaviour'. *Educational Studies*, 12.

Purkey, W.W. (1967) 'The self in academic achievement'. Florida Educational Research and Development Council, *Research Bulletin*, 3,1.

Rosenberg, M.J., Nelson, C. and Vivekanathan, P.S. (1968) 'A multidimensional approach to the structure of personality impression'. *Journal of Personality and Social Psychology*, 9, 283–94.

Rosenthal, R. and Jacobson, L. (1968) *Pygmalion in the Classroom*. New York: Holt, Reinhart and Winston.

Thompson, T. (1994) 'Self-worth protection: review and implications for the classroom'. *Educational Review*, 46, 3, 259–274.

Totman, R. (1982) 'Philosophical foundations of attribution therapies', in C.Antaki and C.Brewin, *Attributions and Psychological Change: Applications of Attributional Theories to Clinical and Educational Practice*. New York: Academic Press.

Weiner, B. (1992) *Human Motivation: Metaphors, Theories and Research*. London: Sage.

Part 3

Experiencing the pressures of learning

Part 3 focuses on the pressures which arise from the organisational, inter-personal and academic features of secondary schooling and how pupils respond to them.

In chapter 9 Chaplain discusses pupils' accounts of what they perceived as stressful and how they coped during their progress through school. There is less research on stress in children than on stress in adults, and what exists is mainly concerned with extreme life-events such as trauma resulting from abuse or from catastrophic/life-threatening episodes. However, it is important to realise that pupils, like adults, may have difficulty coping with the cumulative effects of everyday hassles, and it is on these that this chapter focuses. The recognition of individual differences in what pupils perceive as stressful is essential in understanding both stress and coping processes. Furthermore, the relationship between the source and availability of social and institutional support is important in understanding pupils' beliefs about their ability to control, or at least to understand, the sources of their stress.

Whereas in the past it was the move into the sixth form that signalled a marked increase in work-related pressures and in the requirement to manage time and tasks for oneself, the pressures now seem to have moved down into years 10 and 11. In chapter 10 – 'Getting serious' – Rudduck focuses on pupils' responses to what they experience as a steep incline in the demands of school work and on the extent to which it invades their personal and family lives. Pupils' comments on revision, on coursework and on sitting examinations provide the core of the chapter. Some pupils were less well prepared for the change than others because they had persuaded themselves that the 'real work' of schooling would not begin until they moved into year 10; as a result they were likely to have underestimated the importance of the continuities of learning in years 7 to 9 and of the importance of building up reliable work habits. Pupils responded differently to the pressures: some adopted strategies that minimised the stress rather than maximised their chances of success in their school work; others found that the clear sense of purpose helped them to work better. It is evident from the data that the nature of the pressure at this stage in their school careers disadvantages some pupils more than others.

CHAPTER 9

Pupils under pressure: coping with stress at school

Roland Chaplain

> *I am always tired, pissed off and have a constant headache, which*
> *results in me being even more pissed off!*

This opening comment came from a girl in year 11 who was sharing her feelings about preparing for her final terms in school. It reflects quite colourfully the language of stress and coping used by young people. She went on to say:

> I hardly spend any time with my family since I am always working. My parents seem to understand and my mum gives me support but they both think I spend too much time working which I have no choice out of. I only really go out on Friday night with my friends and sometimes I am even too tired from a week's work. Recently I have worked non-stop for the whole weekend, spending 11 hours on Sunday on a Geography project without stopping for lunch and only with short breaks.

Despite feeling this way she was still positive about her achievements at school ('I am happy with the work I have done') but then continued:

> I have become really depressed with my life since it seems too boring and I don't ever have anything to look forward to. I don't even want to go skiing in half term with my family, which I love doing, as I am worried about how I will get all my work done. Holidays are just for work and so they just seem worse than school time. If I am not working I am worrying about the work I should be doing. So I get depressed and the pressure is just too much. Quite often I cry if I am scared about something and think about what is the point? I don't think that the teachers realise how close many of my friends [mainly girls] come to killing themselves. I think that many people just want to give up. The only thing which I think about is getting good GCSE grades and I can't look any further.

Most studies of stress in schools focus on teachers, and there is a wealth of data available but, as Dunham (1989, p.16) said, 'stress in pupils has aroused less specific concern', even though school-related stress has a considerable influence on children's lives (see Schultz and Heuchert, 1983). Where studies of young people have been carried out, the emphasis has tended to be on their reactions to extreme events (see, for example, Gamezy, 1986). Interesting and important as such studies might be, they offer little to teachers in classrooms dealing with children who are coping with the hassles of everyday life.

In relation to studies of teachers' work we know that not all stress is linked to extreme events and researchers have recognised the importance of the cumulative effects of stress. Disruptive behaviour is a major source of stress (see Borg, 1990) and, as the Elton Report (1989) indicates, teachers' concern about disruption relates mainly to everyday minor behaviours (such as talking out of turn) rather than to serious misbehaviours. The argument of this chapter is that the phenomenon of stress is similar for pupils. Antonovosky (1979) suggested three key sources of stress: cataclysmic life events, major life events and daily hassles. While some young people may experience cataclysmic or major life events in their out-of-school lives and occasionally in their in-school lives, they are as vulnerable as teachers to stress resulting from everyday difficulties. Young people are able to talk about feelings associated with stress and how they try and cope with it. They know when they feel upset or angry, fed up or worried. These commonsense understandings are important because they give us an authentic insight into the structure of stress whereas more rigorous research-based definitions can circumscribe the phenomena. The language young people use to describe stress is, not surprisingly, different from that of their teachers. They talk about being 'stressed out' and they talk about people 'bugging you'; some people 'wind them up' or make them 'upset' and these phrases are associated with feelings of anger. In contrast, the term 'fed up' usually relates to feelings of depression or helplessness (see Chaplain and Freeman, 1994); it is an umbrella term which can reflect a range of feelings – from being tired and unwilling to a state of clinical depression. Adults' interpretations of what children mean when they say they are 'fed up' can be inaccurate.

In one of our satellite studies (see chapter 8) a group of male pupils identified as disengaged and on the whole underachieving were asked whether and how often they felt fed up in school. 22% said that they felt this way all or most of the time and 69% were fed up some of the time. The latter responses were often qualified by statements such as: 'it depends on...'; the evidence suggested that it can depend on the subject, the teacher, examinations and whether things happening outside school are impinging on their work and relationships in school. Such a picture is familiar rather than novel. What was perhaps of most concern was that 42% of the sample of disengaged male pupils said that they first started to feel fed up with school when they were at their primary schools.

Adults' ratings of the nature and severity of stress experienced by children often differ markedly from the ratings made by the children themselves (see, for example, Yamamoto and Felsenthal, 1982). Attempting to find explanations for other people's experiences can mask complex emotional issues. The developmental dynamics of adolescence are often seen by adults – including professionals – as a time when behaviour patterns can be put down to 'hormones' or 'natural challenges to authority'; people say, 'It's just a phase they're going through' and adults commonly believe that adolescents 'will grow out of it'. Such perceptions may lead adults, including teachers, to become less of a source of support or a buffer from stress than young people desire.

To illustrate the scale of stress in secondary school populations at a national level, a recent survey of 13,000 teenagers aged between 13 and 15 years from 65 schools in England and Wales revealed that 53% often felt depressed and had feelings of low self-worth. A further 16% admitted to feelings of loneliness. Just under a quarter of the boys and under a third of the girls said that they had contemplated suicide (Francis and Kay, 1995); such statistics give cause for serious concern.

Stress, coping and social support

Lazarus and Folkman (1984) argue that stress results from a transaction between the appraisals made by individuals and the environment in which they find themselves. The appraisal is in three stages: first, whether or not the potential stressor represents a *threat* to the individual; second, what response is required in order to cope; and third, reappraisal of the effectiveness of the coping response adopted. Chaplain and Freeman (1994) argue that many of our coping strategies are activated automatically, and are made up of responses which we 'overlearn' (by repeated use) as we develop. Stress occurs when we become consciously aware of having to cope – that our automatic systems are not working. In their model the relationship between stress and coping is made explicit. However, while individuals develop ways of coping effectively using their own psychological and physical resources, they are also dependent on support from their social environment (for example, school organisation) and the availability of social support (friends and family). In simple terms *what you do to cope* depends on the interaction between *what you are* and *who you perceive is available to help you.*

Part of coping effectively at a personal level requires individuals to have a self-confident belief in their ability to deal with a range of stressors. Self-efficacy is concerned with individuals' belief in their competence to accomplish specific tasks – a basic need to feel effective in their interactions with the world. An individual's level of self-efficacy is a useful predictor of ability to cope with stress (see Jerusalem and Schwarzer, 1992). Individuals with a low sense of self-efficacy tend to have low self-esteem, are anxious and feel helpless; in contrast, those with a high sense of self-efficacy tend to undertake more challenging tasks and they expect to succeed. This is of particular relevance to teachers, since children with a low sense of perceived control over their lives are unhappy, anxious and eventually become depressed. The salience of self-efficacy in the context of this chapter will become clear.

We know that individuals differ in their reactions to events commonly thought to be stressful. We are also aware of how we cope better at different times of the day and on some occasions better than others, something which research into stress (Chaplain and Freeman, 1994) finds very difficult to explain:

> It is not simply that as individuals we find different experiences more or less stressful, but also we may vary considerably in our capacities to cope with broadly similar situations. (p.16)

Social support is recognised as an important component in helping individuals to cope with stress. Recent research has suggested that different types of social support are appropriate for helping people to cope with different types of stress, including emotional, self-esteem and instrumental (see Cutrona and Russell, 1990). An awareness of the most appropriate type of support and how to provide it is important to teachers concerned about helping young people to develop effective coping strategies. Schools provide different types of support through, for instance, institutional frameworks such as rules and rituals; through interpersonal support from teachers and other pupils (including emotional support from pastoral care and friendship, self-esteem support through recognition of personal worth, and instrumental support such as help with learning). To be effective, however, it is essential for the support to be perceived as *available* and *appropriate* by the pupils.

This chapter focuses on pupils' accounts from the *Making Your Way Through Secondary School* study (see chapter 1) of their experiences of stress and how they cope. The data suggest two broad bases for analysing stress and coping: 'institutional' and 'interpersonal'. Institutional sources of stress will be discussed in terms of:

- Structural – pressure generated by school organisation and management including policies, facilities and rules;
- Curriculum – subject demands, workload and teaching styles.

Interpersonal sources of stress will be discussed in relation to:

- Teacher-pupil relationships;
- Peer-group relationships.

The data will be used to illustrate the relationship between the sources of stress in schools (in the form of everyday hassles), the nature and availability of social support for pupils, and differences in the way potential sources of stress are appraised by pupils and the effects of this appraisal on pupils' self-efficacy.

Institutional stress and support

We recognise that in any organisation some people will experience pressure some of the time. In secondary schools pupils are in transition, both in terms of their academic learning and their social development. When they join a secondary school they move from a social frame based on the classroom to a frame based on the school as a whole. As they progress through school pupils often experience, particularly moving from year 8 to year 9, some sense of the contradictory nature of institutional life: they are told that because they are older they should act more responsibly – 'All the teachers have been telling us how we've got to be more ready for work...we should set examples to, like, the year 7s' (Y9, M) – and yet at the same time they have to conform to seemingly trivial rules.

Of course, institutional structures are designed to provide safe, secure and predictable frameworks for the pupils to help them to cope. Gaining a balance between care and control and learning is difficult, as Emler (1993, p.246) points out: '...Doing well at school could...be a function of the child's adjustment to the peculiar requirements of the bureaucratic regime which he or she encounters there, accommodation to the routine and discipline of a formal timetable and to the authority of teachers'.

Rules, rituals and routines

Pupils in years 7 and 8 were aware of the differences in institutional requirements between themselves and older pupils. Many year 8 pupils said things like this: 'You get more privileges in the upper school...here it's like a cage' (Y8,F); 'Yeah and you have to lock your coat up...and you're not allowed to get it at lunch time...That means in winter you have to freeze to death...because they won't unlock the doors. That's stupid' (Y8,F). They were also apprehensive about asking teachers to unlock doors because '[teachers] don't like doing it, because it's a lot of bother'(Y8,M). From the school's perspective (and from the pupils' when they understand what is at stake) security is an important issue. In many settings the response is to identify secure zones but this strategy could create other difficulties for the young people whom the school is trying to protect. Pupils were aware of such issues: 'You either leave your coat in the cloakroom where it gets nicked or in a classroom, and then you can't go back in the classroom to get it'(Y8,F). These were tensions which pupils wanted eliminated and they themselves came up with a solution: 'We've been asking for lockers lately'(Y8,F), a change that would allow them some degree of autonomy while at the same time providing security.

Feeding large groups of people simultaneously can also generate stress – for both the provider and consumer. Pupils commented quite frequently on the organisation of school dinner which was not always experienced as a pleasant social occasion: 'the dinner system's stupid...you have to eat your dinner in two seconds and get back to class'(Y8,F). Some pupils, in the same school, could not understand why, if they are 'swamped in the dining room', there was a rule about 'not eating outside': as one commented, 'It is a bit stupid'. The lunch-time wait was not seen as stressful by all pupils. For some it had an enjoyable and social aspect: 'We all sit round in a circle...trying each other's shoes on...it's right good. We all like the dinner lady' (Y8,M).

Freedom of movement around school can be hierarchical, and pupils often perceived the rules as unjust: 'I felt angry about things...pupils aren't allowed to go through the main doors, we have to go all the way around' (Y9,M). There were other comments about movement restrictions: 'There are up and down stairs; you go up one side and down the other...[if you]...find you're in the wrong place...[then]...you have to go all the way around again'. Whereas pupils were restricted, 'teachers can just go anywhere they want. It just seems a bit annoying' (Y9,F). Poorly-maintained facilities can be a source of stress for some pupils. In one school, for example, the building itself was depressing: 'It's horrible; all the walls are shabby and tables are falling apart' (Y8,F). In another school badly-maintained toilets caused some distress: 'They are always dirty and there are no locks on the doors...you have to bring a friend with you to hold the door' (Y8,F). However, despite many of the small hassles that the institution generated, at a comparative level this school provided security and support for many of its pupils which was recognised and appreciated, 'It's better than... [other school]...which is...horrible...Everyone [there] smokes and swears' (Y8,M).

Curriculum organisation and teaching style

As they move through school, changes to the organisation of the curriculum can create stress for pupils. They may also feel uncertain about the social support that is available from teachers. In the primary school pupils had one teacher for most of their lessons whom they knew well. At secondary school, however, they may have a form tutor who does not teach them ('you don't really know them that well; they are just registering you'); they can also be bewildered by the fact that 'teachers write reports on you...[and]...you can tell they don't actually know you' (Y9,F). During year 9 the increased pressure of work began to become more of an issue for many children; at the same time they felt teachers demanded more in terms of their conduct: 'Teachers are more strict...' but behave so because they are 'worried about you for next year' (Y9,M).

In year 9, as they moved towards options, they were aware of the potential loss of social support from established friends placed in other groups:

> Like on a Wednesday we have got Technology lessons all morning and where our class is split in half, so some of my friends I don't see all morning. And then after lunch I have got Spanish and then German and then, I think, Maths and they are in a different Maths set. And so you see them for about ten minutes in the morning and then you see them at lunch times and break times but that is about it. (Y9,M)

Some pupils found that having to join different groups placed demands on their interpersonal skills and was a source of considerable anxiety: 'I am scared that I don't know who is going to be in my class' (Y9,F). There were changes to the way in which subjects are taught, 'You get separated from your class, you're in different sets' (Y9,M). It is worth noting that social support groups are often affected by academic status. Established social groups can disappear as a result of organisational structures, such as 'setting'. These divisions can be exacerbated by teachers who unwittingly, or otherwise, relate differently to groups perceived as high or low achievers (see chapter 8). For some, 'setting' signalled an inevitable, and not always welcome, change in social groupings which created crossed loyalties: pupils had to decide whether to identify with friends or to be 'more respectful to the teachers'(Y9,M) in order to stay in the top set. Sets also served to separate former friends and thereby potentially removed a source of social support: 'We don't see each other much because they are in lower sets' (Y9,M). A clear distinction between 'more able' and 'less able' pupils became more apparent in year 9 interviews. Some comments reflected inferences pupils were making about their position in the academic and social order. One pupil, when discussing the effect on individuals of being labelled as being in the lowest set, questioned the need for five categories of ability: 'We shouldn't have so many sets'. More sets meant you could be lower down the ladder, like descending the steps to a dark basement: 'Because kids boast and stuff when you're in the fifth set'. His solution was to reduce the number of 'steps': to have 'one top one, one second and one third for the bad people' (Y9,M) – but clearly the stigma of being in the lowest set would remain.

However, feelings about setting were individualised, which meant different perceptions of the source and availability of social support. For some of the more able pupils, separating classes on the basis of ability was perceived as fair and supportive: 'I think it is a good thing...'cos some people haven't the ability...'(Y10,M). Furthermore, it relieved pressure on the less able and helped them to cope: 'People with limited ability weren't getting anywhere – our teacher likes to push them hard...they didn't pick it up...Now they're in a lower set' (Y9,M). However, some pupils in the higher sets felt that pupils placed in lower sets would consider it an unpleasant experience which would lower their self-esteem: 'They think it's really bad and that they are rubbish'(Y9,F).

Being in a higher set and being confident of maintaining a place there had, not surprisingly, a positive effect on self-worth, a feeling that you are highly valued by teachers: 'I think you are thought better of...by teachers' (Y9,F). For others the pressure of maintaining a place in the top set created anxiety, since failure in *one* exam could result in setting off an unwelcome chain of events. You would receive inferior quality teaching – 'you won't get taught as well' – which would inevitably lead to overall failure 'that will affect basically the rest of your school life' (Y9,M).

However, feelings associated with being in a lower set were also varied and not necessarily negative. For some, there was some relief in being grouped with others of similar ability since it lessened the threat to their social identity: 'Last year...we were with...right brainy people and Mr [teacher] went right fast...but this year we're all t' same' (Y9,F). For others it was viewed as embarrassing and humiliating. Appraising the effects of 'setting' as stressful or supportive was clearly subject to individual differences, particularly for those in the lower sets. It is important to say that being in the lower set was, for some pupils, a respite from the pressure of learning in environments where they felt disadvantaged because of their own perceived lack of ability or their teachers' lack of awareness of, or inability to address, their individual learning needs.

While the content and style of teaching in almost all subjects was criticised by at least one pupil, modern languages attracted many of the most negative responses. Most of the criticism was in the form of angry comments about not understanding what was going on, of helplessness and humiliation. The following comment exemplifies the tone of the responses:

> I don't understand this and you know I'm just sat there with a blank page most of the time and I have to wait for her to come over and tell her that I don't understand. That can be a bit embarrassing sometimes. (Y9,M)

General dissatisfaction with how pupils were taught included lessons that were lacklustre: teachers whose teaching style made the subject seem 'boring', or were themselves perceived as a 'boring person'. Being bored with your work led to a lack of activity which Dunham (1984) suggests is often as likely to generate stress as is overwork. For a few, this feeling extended to all aspects of schooling: 'It's just boring. I hate all the lessons and I don't want to come' (Y10,F). This statement came from a pupil who had enjoyed school up until year 10. She went on to admit to coping with boredom by truanting, although, having been caught, restricted this to lessons rather than whole days, which made it harder to detect. Coping with being bored included both active responses, such as being disruptive ('everyone just messes around'), and passive responses, such as avoidance ('wagging school'), but such off-task activity was not necessarily viewed by the pupils as a positive outcome. Most expressed a desire to learn but felt their access was denied because of teachers' inability to teach effectively, or because of their own lack of self-efficacy, which the teacher was there to help them develop.

A number of pupils expressed anxiety and frustration about teachers perceived as reluctant or unable to teach effectively: 'He doesn't know what he's talking about' (Y9,F). Where this happened, the comments were far more explicit and appeared to indicate a feeling of being prevented from learning and/or being treated unjustly; this made pupils feel angry:

> He doesn't really explain anything. He mutters under his breath so no one knows what to do. (Y9,M)

> He'll write on the board and talk about something, and he'll say 'Right. You can start now'...Usually no-one knows what you're supposed to be starting...He's not even nice about it. (Y9,F)

Pupils offered suggestions as to what teachers should do in order to relieve stress and help them cope with learning in schools:

> I'd sack [teacher] to start with. I'd try to make sure that all teachers can actually teach...that everyone's got an interesting way of teaching...not necessarily the same way...but...to get all the ideas across. (Y9,F)

Stress and support from interpersonal relationships

The importance of social support for adolescents, from their social environments and social connectedness, has been acknowledged as providing a buffer from the effects of stress and for enhancing their self-esteem (see Hirsch et al., 1990).

Teachers

The responsibility teachers have, or should have, to provide social support is very evident in the comments of the pupils. For some pupils, it was the perceived lack of support from teachers which caused them most stress: 'You get up in a morning and think, God I can't handle school today...it's not so much the lessons but the teachers' (Y9,F). While adolescence is often viewed as a period of adult de-idealisation (see Steinberg and Silverberg, 1986), young people continue to turn to adults for advice and social support. As we saw earlier, pupils expect teachers to take an active interest in them as human beings and they can feel more susceptible to stress and anxiety if this does not happen. Teachers' interest in their well-being appears to be an important ingredient of many pupils' social networks and, more especially, support. To many pupils taking an active interest means treating them with respect. By year 8 they were quick to criticise teachers who did not treat them with respect: 'Well, some teachers talk to you as if you are really inferior to them' (Y8, M). Believing significant others perceive and treat you as inferior has a direct and negative effect on self-image and self-efficacy, and hence on coping. This pupil went on to explain *how* some teachers distanced themselves from him and treated him as inferior and irrelevant: 'They just don't get to know you, they just read out instructions'. Pupils expected teachers to make an effort, to take the time to communicate what was required of them and to have a human touch: 'I don't like his attitude to the class...He's not friendly and he won't help you' (Y9,F). Some teachers, it appeared, in attempting to communicate with and support pupils, fell foul of invading pupils' private space by trying to be 'streetwise' – as one pupil put it, trying 'to speak with the same kind of words that *pupils* use', which resulted in them 'ending up looking stupid'. These failed attempts to be 'with it' in order to communicate and support have been observed elsewhere (Chaplain and Freeman, 1994). Pupils often view this as unacceptable since it undermines their expectations of teachers' authority.

Pupils' self-efficacy can be reduced by teachers' attempts to enhance motivation. Comparison between classes is often used by teachers to develop a sense of 'healthy competition'. Research has shown, however, that for some groups, usually those who perceive themselves as lacking academic ability, such comparison can have the detrimental effect of lowering their self-image and reducing their efforts. For one of our groups, comparison with another class by a particular teacher was perceived as de-motivating:

> She always says we are rubbish and we never do anything well...all she ever says is 'the other group has done this...and you are *just* doing this, aren't you rubbish?' I don't think people will respond to it. (Y9,F)

In some cases, pupils' self-perceptions become so low they develop learned helplessness (see Seligman, 1975) which is characterised by behaviours such as difficulty in coping, depression, and a belief that they have little ability. Effort is of no use since they do not feel in control of their lives. The development of learned helplessness is a cause for concern since it is hard to break once established and has been found to continue into adult life.

For some pupils in our study, certain teachers created an unsupportive negative climate in their classrooms. Telling groups of pupils that they are 'the most boring to teach' was reciprocated by pupils 'being less willing to talk to her anyway' (Y9,F). Such behaviour is likely to maintain a negative feedback cycle. The consequences are that both teachers and pupils experience stress through reduced mutual support.

Peers

As pupils move through their secondary education peers begin to occupy a more central role in their lives. Peers provide social support in times of distress or when individuals are in conflict with adults. But, in contrast, they can also be a source of stress through bullying or social isolation. Young people are under pressure to conform to the conduct rules of teachers and of peers, which may conflict (see Emmerich et al., 1971). For some pupils there are difficulties in maintaining their relationships with and support from adults and children without 'betraying' one or both. This could lead to them isolating themselves from both, thereby exacerbating their difficulties:

I don't get on with my family anymore, they think I'm being a moody teenager...I'm not! What I'm doing in my bedroom is working...the only time I see my friends out of school is on Friday night...I often think I have no life and...there is no point carrying on. I don't think teachers understand what we are going through and have little sympathy for us. (Y11,F)

It was evident from comments by pupils in this study that their peer support was often inconsistent. However, during early adolescence at least, many pupils have limited social insight and social comprehension and this can lead to communication difficulties and misinterpretation of other people's motivational intent. As a result, pupils 'fall in and out of relationships' (Erikson, 1968). Girls seemed particularly vulnerable:

They [Ester and Natasha] are right horrible. And now Jean [a former friend] says she's not going to hang around with me and Anne, Joan and Glynis any more. She's going to hang around with Ester and Natasha. (Y8,F)

We don't like her because she sucks...she came back to us but then she went back to [another group of girls]...they told her what they thought of her so she came back to us. We wouldn't mind if she hung around with us all of the time but she keeps hopping around. (Y8,F)

Some pupils suffered an assault on their self-image when openly mocked in the classroom by more academically able groups: 'They were right horrible saying, "Oh we don't work with yaw" [mock posh accent]...they treat us like we're really stupid' (Y8,F). Others perceived their more capable peers as selfish in not providing instrumental support by sharing their knowledge and skills: 'They all hang around together and they never help us, because they are the brainy ones' (Y9,F).

Sadly, for some there seems to be no one to whom they feel they can turn for social support: 'I really hate everybody else in that class. They are the most boring people I've ever met in my life'(Y10,M). While it might be easy to discard such a statement as reflecting a temporary state, for a few, social isolation – self-inflicted or otherwise – can be a profoundly disturbing issue and lead to feelings of hopelessness. Social isolation as a consequence of limited social competence and anxiety has been recognised by educational researchers, most recently through research into victims of bullying (see Stephenson and Smith, 1989).

Improving schools to improve pupil coping

In this chapter we have examined the balance between the sources of stress and support for coping offered to pupils through school structures and interpersonal relationships. We have emphasised the importance of recognising individual appraisal when attempting to determine whether or not an event is perceived as stressful. Schools differ in their ability to provide the optimal conditions to help pupils to cope with stress; some are clearly more effective than others in this respect. Schools which generate stress for pupils may do so as a result of attempting to provide safe and efficient places to work and learn. Many of the institutional structures which pupils in this study perceived as stressful were introduced by adults who genuinely believed they were acting in the pupils' best interests. The stress generated is an unintended consequence. However, it is inevitable that in managing large institutions there will be some conflicts between providing for the needs of the individual and the needs of the institution. It is essential, therefore, that the intended functions of a structure are made explicit to all those involved.

In an earlier study (see Chaplain and Freeman, 1994) we asked pupils and staff in one institution about their understanding of the meaning of various everyday routines, such as lining up before meals, pastoral counselling and reward systems. We found that the two groups had very different interpretations of the meanings of these routines. Lining up, for example, was perceived by pupils as making them feel safe, whereas the staff saw it as a mechanism for exercising control over the group. Where there is a lack of shared understanding of the intended function of a school structure, it is likely to generate stress for both parties.

Secondary schools are organised around an examination system, the salience of which is transmitted formally and tacitly from early on in a pupil's career, and school structures reflect this. To maximise learning pupils are often 'setted' which we have shown can remove an important source of social support. In some cases pupils saw it as divisive and harmful to relationships and this could lead to the creation of subcultures that provided the social support denied by the formal institution. Given current concerns about school attendance and social behaviour, it seems reasonable to ask if the unintended consequences of such structures need to receive more attention.

Our pupils made it clear what they expected from teachers to improve their coping and learning. They had to take an interest, teach competently and have good professional social skills. The message was clear from both high and low attainers, although they differed in what they believed needed changing. Teachers are an important part of pupil social support but to help pupils develop effective coping they need to be sensitive to the conflicting and wide-ranging pressures on pupils from their parents, peers and other teachers. One of the difficulties in providing social support is that inactive, depressive and ungrateful people, those most in need, are seen as the least socially attractive (see chapter 8). As a consequence, this group tends to receive less support from others. In schools this group can include less able, aggressive and socially withdrawn pupils. Their behaviour tends to make the provider frustrated and helpless and less likely to want to give support; they also receive negative messages from teachers and peers, both of which can exacerbate an already low level of self-perception (see Dunkel-Schetter and Wortman, 1981).

While some of these difficulties can be overcome by pupils' developing their personal coping styles and social competence, there is a clear message for teachers. Although pastoral systems usually provide social support, *all* teachers can play an important role in providing an appropriate balance of instrumental and emotional support to pupils to enhance their self-efficacy and outcome expectancies, and thereby enhance coping.

References

Antonovosky, A. (1979) *Health, Stress and Coping*. San Francisco: Jossey Bass.

Borg, M.G. (1990) 'Occupational stress in British educational settings: a review'. *Educational Psychology*, **10**,2, 103–126.

Chaplain, R. and Freeman, A. (1994) *Caring Under Pressure*. London: David Fulton Publishers.

Cutrona, C. and Russell, D. (1990) 'Types of social support and specific stress: towards a theory of optimal matching', in I.G. Sarason, B.R. Sarason and G.R. Pierce (eds) *Social Support: An Interactional View*. New York: Wiley.

Dunham, J. (1984) *Stress in Teaching*. London: Croom Helm.

Dunham, J. (1989) 'Stress management – relaxation and exercise for pupils in secondary schools'. *Pastoral Care in Education*, **7**, 2, 16–20.

Dunkel-Schetter, C. and Wortman, C. B. (1981) 'Dilemmas of social support: parallels between victimisation and ageing', in I.B. Keisler, J.N. Morgan and V.K. Oppenheimer (eds) *Ageing: Social Change*. New York: Academic Press.

Elton Report (1989) *Discipline in Schools*. London: HMSO.

Emler, N. (1993) 'The young person's relationship to the institutional order', in S. Jackson and H. Rodriguez-Tome (eds) *Adolescence and its Social Worlds*. Hove: Lawrence Erlbaum Associates.

Emmerich, W., Goldman, K.S. and Shore, R. E. (1971) 'Differentiation and development of social norms'. *Journal of Personality and Social Psychology*, **18**, 323–353.

Erikson, E.H. (1968) *Identity: Youth and Crisis*. New York: W.W. Norton.

Francis, L.J. and Kay, W.K. (1995) *Teenage Religion and Values*. Leominster: Gracewing.

Gamezy, N. (1986) 'Children under severe stress: critique and commentary'. *Journal of the American Academy of Child Psychiatry*, **25**, 3, 384–392.

Hirsch, B.J., Engel-Levy, A., DuBois, D.L. and Hardesty, P.H. (1990) 'The role of the social environment in social support', in B.R. Sarason, I.G. Sarason, and G.P. Pierce, (eds) *Social Support: An Interactional View*. New York: Wiley.

Jerusalem, M. and Schwarzer, R. (1992) 'Self-efficacy as a resource factor in stress appraisal processes', in R. Schwarzer (ed.) *Self-Efficacy: Thought Control of Action*. Washington: Hemisphere.

Lazarus, R.S. and Folkman, S. (1984) *Stress, Appraisal and Coping.* New York: Springer Publishing.

Schultz, E.W. and Heuchert, C.M. (1983) *Child Stress and the School Experience.* New York: Human Sciences Press.

Seligman, M.E.P. (1975) *Helplessness: On Depression, Development and Death.* San Francisco: Freeman Press.

Steinberg, L. and Silverberg, S.B. (1986) 'The vicissitudes of autonomy in early adolescence'. *Child Development,* **67**, 841–851.

Stephenson, P. and Smith, P. (1989) 'Bullying in the junior school', in D.Tattum and D. Lane (eds) *Bullying in Schools.* Stoke on Trent: Trentham Books.

Yamamoto, K. and Felsenthal, H.M. (1982) 'Stressful experiences of children: professional judgements. *Psychological Reports,* **50**, 1087–1093.

CHAPTER 10:

Getting serious: the demands of coursework, revision and examinations[1]

Jean Rudduck

The five-year span of compulsory secondary schooling is unlike any other period of formal education in the sharpness of its transitions. Year 7 is the year of joining the 'big school' and getting to know the ropes. Years 8 and 9 are a period, for most pupils, of social exploration; no longer the youngest in the school, they stretch out towards the edges of their autonomy – and they also try out new friendships. Years 10 and 11, in the pupils' eyes, are about the 'real work' of schooling – and it is during these two years that pupils also become increasingly conscious of themselves as learners and future workers. A recurrent theme in our data for these two years is the relationship between the pressures of school work and pupils' strategies for coping.

Where once (see Rudduck and Hopkins, 1984) it was the move into the sixth form that signalled a marked increase in work-related pressures and demands, now it is the move into years 10 and 11 that opens up a new order of seriousness and a new set of tensions. While coursework itself relates reasonably clearly to pupils' previous experiences of topic and project work, they have little experience of the organisation and management techniques required to construct portfolios of coursework to deadlines, nor have they much experience of formal examinations and associated revision skills. How then do they manage the transition from the relatively relaxed pace – as they see it – of the first three years of secondary school to the very different pace and purposes of GCSE work?

The message about the need 'to work hard for your exams' is strongly transmitted by teachers and by many parents and older siblings (see also chapters 6 and 12). Sometimes the message is relayed in years 7 and 8 as a device for settling pupils into good work habits early in their school career, as the following statement from a year 8 pupil suggests: 'Some of the teachers are saying that if you waste time at start of lessons and you add up all that time, like if you waste ten minutes [each lesson], it's going to add up to a year of work gone and you'll do badly in your GCSEs' (Y8,F). For others, the message only really gains significance at the start of year 10, or a little later, when the pressures begin to bite: 'Well, I know like this year and next year are the most important years and I've got to cram everything in' (Y10,F). Even pupils who have been irregular attenders feel the need to change their ways: 'I am attending all the time because you need to study for your exams' (Y11,M). And pupils who have in the past missed school for minor ailments – as the following pupil had done – now think twice about being absent:

> There's a lot of pressure on you now. It's like if you don't do well now you're not going to do well in GCSEs. Like if you're ill you're right scared of missing like some maths and, like, I had a problem with my arm, my right arm, so I was really useless at being in school and stuff and my mum said, 'Well, why don't you stay at home?' and I can't because I've got my science lesson and I have a science test. (Y10,F)

Where pupils have clear horizons they can develop a stronger sense of purpose. On a small scale, modules and tests offer short-term goals which many pupils find helpful and the year 11 targets also offer a clear if longer-term view ahead, or, to use Silberman's (1971) metaphor, an important experience of 'direction' and 'navigation'. As one pupil said: 'I've got this big goal in front of me and I'll be ready to work for it when I get back to school [i.e. after the holiday]' (Y10,F).

There is a shared rhetoric that virtually all pupils accept: you've got to work hard to get qualifications so that you get a good job (see chapter 11). Some pupils know that they have not worked well up to now and that their foundations for the 'harder' work of years 10 and 11 are shaky; others, however, see years 10 and 11 as a self-contained period of study that they can opt into – suddenly changing their attitude to school work and the way they work. The fact that new subjects (options) *do* start in year 10 may strengthen the idea that this is a self-contained stage and that what has gone before was not only different in kind but also that it didn't matter too much – as this pupil optimistically explained: 'It's a new year so you can start from scratch and now I'm thinking of, like, moving up sets...It would be a new start and I could work harder...'(Y10,M).

The pressures and the tensions

The pressure seems to build quite dramatically – although work experience, at the end of year 10 or the start of year 11, is a strange interlude, leading some pupils to increase their efforts to work hard for the sake of qualifications and others to relax their efforts and to settle, if they can, for something at the end of the year that won't require too many qualifications. The overall impression from our interviews, however, is that in year 11 most pupils want to do well and are trying (although not all are succeeding) to manage the various demands of school work and home and social life. 'Year 11 is the most stressful year', they say – and the sense of stress is sometimes acute, as the following comments suggest:

> I come home from school, do work, watch 'Home and Away' and 'Neighbours', then work. Eat my tea and work, go to bed and have nightmares about GCSE results. What a life! (Y11,F)

> The only time I see my friends out of school is Friday night...basically I have no life and I often think there is no point in carrying on because life is so boring...I'm not too worried about doing my exams but the amount of work involved now is too much and I'm finding it hard to cope. (Y11,F)

> If I do go out I feel guilty as though I should be revising or doing some project work. (Y11,F)

> Because of all the stress that was put on us our headteacher said that we shouldn't be given homework over the Christmas holidays but teachers ignored this and gave us still just as much to do so I spent the Christmas holidays working. (Y11,F)[2]

The language of the last statement suggests that the pressure is constructed 'by others' – and it is usually teachers who are blamed:

> The teachers don't understand that we have other subjects and not just the ones they teach. (Y11,F)

> I don't think that teachers understand. They all presume that there is nothing else for you to do except their subject. They don't realise there are 11 other subjects from which you also get the same enormous amounts of work. (Y11,M)

Pupils need, at this stage in their lives, not only to maintain their social networks (especially with friends they don't go to school with) but also, as some put it, 'time to themselves now and then'. At the same time, some pupils are beginning to accept that the responsibility, and the choice whether to work hard or not, is theirs. Many pupils say that they are not enjoying year 11 because of the pressures and because learning is 'not as much fun as it was before' (Y11,F). Others say that what they like about year 11 is the focusing of the work and knowing that it is important. And there is the occasional phlegmatic voice saying, 'Well, I suppose it's doing us good really because we need it all for us GCSEs...'(Y10,F).

While most of the pupils quoted above have decided to give priority to school work whatever the cost, others are intent on developing a strategy that reflects their prioritisation of social over academic activities:

> I have a strict programme for homework and revision. At 7.00pm every Monday to Thursday nights I do one and a half hours...On Fridays I do one hour as soon as I get home from school and then I do not do anything all day Saturdays or Sunday...This routine means that my school work does not interfere at all with my private life. (Y11,M)

> My school work fits into the gaps in my life, not the other way round. If there's something I want to do or someone I want to see I will do it or see them. My work fits into the spare moments. I figure that if I'm not enjoying my life I might as well be dead so I'll enjoy it as much as I can and school work is something to do in my spare time. (Y11,M)

There seems to be a range of attitudes in each form group – although, as the selection of quotations suggests, there are some clear gender differences in the pattern of response to the pressures. On the whole, most female pupils are prepared to get on with the work but there is a minority of male pupils who seek protection from working hard in peer-support groups whose attitude is characterised by anti-work norms and a display of public nonchalance (see also chapter 8). What makes it difficult for them is that whereas once their antics may have been enjoyed by their peers, now there is a tendency among those who are trying to do well to reject those who disrupt learning and take teachers' time and attention away from supporting their own learning.

Coursework, exams and revision

Coursework[3]

Coursework is something that, usually, goes into a portfolio which is formally assessed and moderated and which contributes to a final GCSE grade. Seeing what a good portfolio should look like can be daunting, as this pupil recalls: 'They've been showing us these folders and they've been right fat and they say yours has got to look like this – and that's hard work' (Y10,M). The amount and nature of coursework varies according to pupils' option choices. Managing coursework portfolios across subjects requires new responsibilities for the organisation of time over and above the challenges of more advanced content. Managing different assignments for different deadlines is a key skill. Pupils must learn to plan and prioritise their work, at home as well as school. They have to take a far greater degree of personal responsibility than had previously been required by homework assignments. Understandably – and advisedly, it seems! – teachers are constantly reminding pupils about the importance of their coursework for their prospects in the GCSE examinations. The problem is that pupils are constantly having to decide what to give their time to; these three pupils are reacting quite differently to similar pressures:

> [In year 10] getting the coursework finished was much more important to me than doing my mock exams. (Y11,F)

> If the work is only homework and not coursework I'll ignore it or do it quickly. If it's coursework I'll do it. (Y11,M)

> At the moment [autumn term] I have massive amounts of coursework from nearly every subject and I still have homework to do as well. I find the coursework takes a back burner as the homework has closer deadlines. (Y11,F)

In these conditions, keeping up is particularly difficult for those pupils whose self-confidence as learners and whose capacity to organise their lives effectively is fragile. Pupils who are not well organised can, as we have seen, mishandle the balancing of time across their school, family and friends. A small number decide to opt out of the struggle: 'There's a few in our form that's settled down in the past year, that's got stuck into their work, but other people just don't care or don't bother coming to school' (Y10,F). Some cope but resent the extent to which school work impinges on out-of-school time, while others learn to manage the various demands and enjoy the feeling of control. Indeed, compared with examinations, coursework allows pupils to work at something over time, to come back to it, to review it and to improve it; such possibilities give pupils a greater sense of ownership of their work:

> I just prefer doing it because you can do it in your own time...I know its got to be in at a certain time but like probably a couple of weeks...[but] you can add to it, and, you know what I mean, like you can pick it up again and like do it again if you want. (Y10,F)

> ...like [you] go to the end like and do an exam and if you fail that you've had it. But if you like have coursework, if you like get one part wrong you can do it again and keep doing it again until you get it like, you know, so you get a good mark for it. (Y10,F)

If we are concerned that pupils develop criteria for judging the quality of their output, then coursework provides an opportunity. However, although coursework gives pupils an important sense of 'ownership', as well as helping to develop a sense of standards, some are acutely aware of the pressure to 'get it done' rather than to take their time and to reflect on and improve their work.

Examinations

With coursework, as we have seen, pupils appreciate having the time to review their work and improve it. In comparison, exams seem very final and, to some, downright unreasonable – urged for many years to 'do their best' many pupils know that they might not be able to produce their best work in conditions which are so time-constrained. Pupils are concerned:

> I get too nervous for [tests and exams]. Coursework is really good for me because it helps me to get a higher grade without doing a test. (Y10,M)

And then there is the perennial fear of anxiety-induced amnesia:

> So, like, I'd memorised all this work and I thought, 'Oh, great, I'm going to do well' and I went in and like I told my boyfriend, I says, 'It's going to go blank my mind, I know it is. I'll not remember anything'. And I go in [to the mocks] and nothing would come to me. (Y10,F)

Part of the problem may well be that exams, through their association with classroom tests, come to be perceived as about the recall and reproduction of information – as a test of memory, which is particularly vulnerable to blanking out – and not of thinking *in situ*. Pupils' approaches to revision bear this out.

Realising how unreal and disorienting an experience it is for many young people to sit on their own, in silence, for a couple of hours, and answer a set of disparate questions – most do their school work and homework in very different conditions – teachers try to familiarise pupils with the setting and the procedures by staging a 'taster' session in year 10 before the full-scale mock exam in year 11. These 'rehearsals' function in part as a mechanism for underlining the formality and seriousness of the situation – although one pupil offered her own theory of the purpose: 'The mocks are just there to scare you into making you work a lot harder. [The real exams are] a lot easier than the mocks' (Y10,F). Although there may be some element of this, teachers are also seeking to demystify the occasion without totally reducing its motivating awe. The experience was seen by pupils as helpful. In one school, for instance, pupils liked the joke which their year tutor had built in as a way of checking whether they had read the instructions properly; it was clear from the interviews that the point had sunk in. Despite the view that the tasters and mocks are there to frighten you, the events in all three schools seem to have been conducted with care and a concern to minimise the anxiety without diminishing pupils' sense of the significance of the event. Indeed, pupils felt better because they knew what to expect – and some even admitted that they quite liked the chance to work in relatively undisturbed silence:

> We had a two hour maths exam and I'd never had a two hour exam before...it was a totally different atmosphere...you had your little desks and you had to take your bags to the front and you had to hand all your pencil cases in [and use] a polythene bag, yes. And it did seem a lot more important. (Y10,F)

[The hall] really looked dark and dull. It looked horrible. But once we got in like we were all going, 'ooh!' Then we started on the first page and we just got stuck into it all right...We had exams like every day. And the first two days we were all nerve-racked and it were horrible sitting there and being quiet, but then I just got used to it. It were all right. (Y10,F)

When you're sat down and everyone's quiet you just want to like stand up and say, 'Somebody talk to me!' It's like just sat there and silent and you don't know what to do and it's like, 'Oh I need help' [but] you can't ask for help. (Y10,F)

I thought, 'Oh no! Got exams today,' and then we'll go upstairs and sit down and it's like you're there and you can do your work and there's no one affecting you because everybody's silent. It were right good. And I've had good results as well in them. (Y10,M)

Some, however, refused to conform even in the examination hall:

There were some lads behind us. Some of the silly lads in the year kept making rude noises and throwing pencils and rulers and spitting at you... [I] felt like getting up and cracking them. (Y10,F)

Pupils vary in their willingness to try to understand new situations in their schooling. While some come to terms with them, others reject them, expressing their uncertainty (or perhaps their sense of inadequacy) through withdrawal or through disruptive behaviour. And sometimes there is a touch of bravado in pupils' attempts to reconcile the tension between the obligation to work hard that the system imposes and the social requirement to be cool and do your own thing (see also chapter 8). Pupils – and our evidence is mostly from male pupils – resolved the dilemma by claiming that exams are easy and don't require much effort in advance:

It works. Did last year. I started off really bad, all I do like in lessons I talk to my mates, but I always get everything down that I know I need and then before any exam, I like revise my socks off and never stop all week...Shock all the teachers...It's brilliant. (Y10,M)

This was an able pupil whom many teachers felt did not work as hard as he could in many classes and his strategy worked – he did achieve his objective. Such strategic planning, which seems to be a resource for the able but laid back, can, of course, breed resentment among peers who are less confident, who work hard and who still don't get good grades. A form tutor comments: 'X is really trying very hard at school and she becomes very despondent at times when she works so hard and produces so much work and she feels as if she's getting nowhere... She referred to a boy in the group who didn't do anything and messes around in half the lessons and he got a B while she got a G. It's hard on her because she is trying so hard.'

Our evidence suggests that some (but not all) pupils began to develop strategies for coping with the demands of examinations. Whereas for coursework the major problem was time management, for examinations it was revising and coping with the somewhat mysterious procedures. As the year proceeded, pupils learned more about the examination system and came to terms with it in their own ways. For some this meant a steady and consistent daily work schedule; for others it meant waiting until the last minute and relying on an intensive burst of revision, buttressed by 'native wit'. Some had advice or practical support from siblings, parents or friends – and some did not.

Revision

One pupil described an exam as like a 'compulsory worksheet' – the paper is put in front of you and whereas you can decide not to do the worksheet, there is a general acceptance that the examination paper requires a response – 'You've *got* to do it' (Y10,F). Revision was seen in the same way; even if pupils found it boring, as many did, they accepted that at some point it had to be done. A researcher (Woods, 1990, p. 155) called it 'socialised instrumentalism', meaning that even when pupils do not enjoy the work they may still do it because they regard it as important:

> I can't be doing revision amongst all the normal school but I *am* doing it. I read through all my work and make flow diagrams. For science I go to after school revision lessons on Tuesdays and Thursdays. I go to German revision on Tuesday lunch times. For maths I found a big book from the public library called, *The Way to Pass GCSE Maths*...I find it easier to learn from that book than I do at school. Revision is boring but to do well it has to be done. (Y11,F)

A number of pupils share this global judgement (i.e., that revision is intrinsically boring) while others make some distinctions – this pupil, for instance: 'I find some revision interesting...but subjects I don't like or I'm struggling with I find boring' (Y11,M). One pupil says that because she finds revision 'sometimes difficult and sometimes boring' she has decided to find a way of making it a bit more interesting. She went on: 'I haven't thought of anything yet, but I will' (Y11,F).

Part of the problem is knowing whether you have to revise everything – 'just going over *all* the work what we've done. That's what I do' (Y10,F) – or whether you should be selective and, if selective, what principle should guide the selection. Pupils who were able to articulate a principle of selection were few; but some were aware of the problem: 'Usually it's like I end up learning big chunks because I don't know like which bits to take out and learn. It's a bit of a problem' (Y10,F). The comments from two other pupils in the same form stood out:

> You've got to sort of think about what you're going to be asked and sort of look at it and think, 'Right, well, that will come in handy and that won't so I'll revise this first. (Y10,F)

> I am revising by reading through all my books, start at year 7 and working my way up to the books I am using now. I have a pad of A4 paper and I write down all the points which I think are important. (Y11,M)

Pupils who find security in being neat and thorough tend merely to aim at learning 'everything' in a systematic way. A female pupil from the same form explained that she read through 'every single page' (Y11,F) and then she thought up recall questions and asked her sister to check the accuracy of her answers. Others concentrate not so much on a strategy that helps directly with their learning, whether selective or unselective, but on making the conditions of revision more acceptable – by taking regular breaks or by listening in to their Walkman at the same time and having a packet of sweets beside them – 'It's relaxing and helps you to concentrate' is the explanation (Y11,F). Teachers help by producing study guides but most pupils are developing their own approaches – and they are varied, both in style and potential reliability:

> What I've done is put everything on tape, and then, when you go to sleep if you listen to it it's supposed to stay in your mind. Tried that. It worked a bit. I forgot a bit of things. (Y10,F)

> And then I just keep giving myself these little tests...and it varies with the different subjects. Maths, I find it impossible to revise for...I think with maths if you don't understand it when you do it you're lost...it's hopeless. (Y10,F)

> I go through all the term's work and check over it, and then write notes down what I need to know. And then I keep repeating them all the time to myself. And then I get my mum or dad to give me a quick test on them, see what I know. And things I don't know I just keep repeating all the time until it gets into my head. (Y10,F)

Another pupil, more productively perhaps, was using a strategy that she had come across in a guide for doing well in the SATs: '[You] sit down, read through your notes – remember the *key words* is what you're supposed to do' (Y10,F).

The evidence suggests that the majority of pupils are tackling the task of revising in their own individual ways but there are some who claim that revision makes them more muddled (perhaps because they do not really understand the nature of the task): 'If I just come straight into a test and do it I usually get better grades. If I revise it muddles me up' (Y10,M). 'If I do too much revising I just forget it all' (Y10,F) – in fact this pupil concludes that the information is unlikely to survive a night's sleep and so it is better to revise 'while I am having my breakfast' or by 'reading it on the way to school'. Again, we see the strength of the view that revision is just learning what is in the text book, or, more often, in the pupil's notebooks, with little critical concern about the quality of the notes constructed, and, it seems, with little reflection on the way that revision might vary from subject to subject – and why. A few pupils are critical – but of the overall procedure: 'I just can't see any point, just going over your work again. I know it's like to remind you but it just gets boring and boring' (Y10,M).

Helping pupils cope with the pressure in years 10 and 11

Some pupils, especially those who were more confident in themselves as learners, liked the sharper sense of focus and purpose in years 10 and 11. But others reacted differently. At first, with the attraction of starting on subjects that they have chosen for themselves and a general sense of a new and altogether more serious phase of work, year 10 may offer pupils who have become disengaged a chance to come back on board. But the steep incline in the demands of school work and homework may prove too much. Some pupils become aware at this stage of their lack of 'scaffolding', in terms of foundations of knowledge and ways of working. Extrinsic motivation (see also chapter 6) may be high but some pupils lack the capacity to analyse their own profile as learners and have difficulty in developing strategies that will serve them well. The strategies described in the responses to our questions reflected different understandings of the nature of the task and, sometimes, different levels of aspiration. Some strategies are designed to reduce stress rather than maximise chances of success: a minority of pupils claimed, for instance, that they would rely on last minute revision to get them through the examinations, while others decided to save face and claimed that they would go for the lowest effort that would secure them moderate success. Public statements of intent (for example, of the 'I'm not bothered' variety) may differ from private hopes as pupils become more keenly aware of the link between qualifications and the labour market.

This is a time when 'coping skills' come into their own. In the face of a barrage of (sometimes contradictory) pressures and (sometimes disturbing) realisations – for some, the realisation that they have left things too late – pupils are trying to hang on to their self-esteem and project a sense of reasonable confidence. Some 'cope' by avoiding the pressure and dropping out – but dropping out, even if the pupils concerned manage to get a job, does not necessarily take away the belief that qualifications and training may after all prove to be a passport to a more confident future. (Because some pupils had dropped out before the end of year 10 their feelings are not well represented in this chapter.) Others cope because they 'get their heads down' and work as hard as they can, knowing that their friends are in the same boat and that the period of pressure has a foreseeable end.

Teachers may be concerned at the way that the framework of pressure disadvantages some pupils more than others. For instance, some pupils may be disadvantaged at this stage in their school careers by lack of access to 'insider' knowledge or 'know-how' (i.e. advice about how best to tackle revision is not available within their family), or by the lack of good conditions, resources and spaces for working at home, or by the non-availability of out-of-school support in subject-related knowledge (for example, some families can afford, and know how to find, subject-specific tutoring for their children). Pupils from families where there is a tradition of academic study are likely to have a greater awareness of the continuities and purposes of learning than pupils from families where parents or carers are more concerned about the 'here and now' needs of daily coping than the deferred benefits of qualifications. And as dividing practices increase in school, and the number of pupils excluded from schools also increases, we see more young people resolving the tension surrounding their own progress and status by accepting the label of 'misfit'. Stevenson and Ellsworth (1993, p. 266) have written about pupils who leave school angry with the system or who construe the situation as one in which they are 'in a good place but unable to succeed', an experience which is easily transformed into what may be a life-long perception that they are just 'not the right kind of person'. The divisions levied by social class continue to have a powerful influence on young people's life chances.

While many of the sources of advantage and disadvantage lie in structures that are beyond the school's reach, there are, nevertheless, some things that can be done to ensure that *all* pupils are well-informed, understand what year 10 and year 11 work entails, and have the best support that the school can reasonably offer. Some of the things that can make a difference at this stage (and we know that many schools already do some or all of them) are these; schools might:

- **help pupils to understand what 'working hard' and 'working harder' means in different subjects**, including what kind of effort it entails for different pupils, and what the pay-offs are;

- **review the focus and coverage of the sessions they run on revision**, to include the rationale for revision, the way in which different subjects or courses may make different demands and the way in which the different learning styles of individual pupils can affect their approach to revision; the strategies commonly adopted by pupils could be discussed and their strengths and weaknesses examined;
- **review with pupils strategies for checking the quality of their own revision notes,** and also the status of revision notes offered by teachers in some subjects, and the status of commercially available revision guides and advice;
- **offer dinner-hour or after school clinics or revision sessions,** where pupils can ask about things they do not understand, catch up on things they have missed, and repeat sequences of work that they cannot grasp but know are important (teachers seem willing to do this even though it means extra work for them);
- **discuss with pupils the problems of managing the multiple demands of coursework, homework and revision,** ensuring that they are well-informed about procedures and requirements, and also being attentive, in the scheduling of tasks and deadlines, to the overall map of demands made by the teachers of the different courses that each pupil is following.

There is a limit, of course, to how much extra effort teachers can put in at a time when they are exhausted by learning the ropes of a new curriculum and assessment system – a system which some think has led to an overload of courses that are not bringing out the best in all their pupils. Nevertheless, many teachers in the schools that took part in the research were finding ways of giving more time to pupils, especially those whose circumstances at home did not make it easy for them to settle to a regime of systematic and orderly revision and those who needed support in escaping the peer-group pressure *not* to be seen to be working hard. And teachers were also responding – through extra-curricular subject-based 'clinics' – to the needs of pupils who wanted to go over those bits and pieces of their work in different subjects that they knew they did not understand. Pupils who had been helped in this way were appreciative of teachers' concern for them and of the more collaborative teaching–learning relationships that were developing at this stage in their school career. Overall, our data show that most pupils genuinely wanted to work hard and to do well – but it's tough being a pupil at key stage 4. It's also pretty tough being a key stage 4 teacher.

Notes

[1]Some passages in this chapter are adapted from Rudduck, J. (1995) and from Harris, S. Wallace, G. and Rudduck, J. (1995).

[2]In the first term of year 11 we invited comments not in interview but through questionnaire and the passages quoted in this chapter are taken from both the year 10 interviews and the year 11 questionnaire responses.

[3]We are aware that the proportion of coursework to examined work has now diminished at key stage 4.

References

Harris, S., Wallace, G. and Rudduck, J. (1995) '"It's not that I haven't learnt much. It's just that I don't really understand what I'm doing": metacognition and secondary school students', *Research Papers in Education*, **10**, 2, 253–271

Rudduck, J. (1995) 'Transitions in the secondary school and their significance for students' commitment to learning', *Education Section Review*, **19**, 2, 69–74.

Rudduck, J. and Hopkins, D. (1984) *The Sixth Form and Libraries*. Library and Information Research Report 24, London: The British Library.

Silberman, M. L. (1971) 'Discussion', in M. L. Silberman (ed.) *The Experience of Schooling*. New York: Holt, Rinehart and Winston.

Stevenson, R. B. and Ellsworth, J. (1993) 'Dropouts and the silencing of critical voices', in L. Weis and M. Fine (eds) *Beyond Silenced Voices: Class, Race and Gender in United States Schools*. New York: SUNY Press, pp. 259–271.

Woods, P. (1990) *The Happiest Days?* Lewes: Falmer Press.

Part 4

Facing the future

For some pupils the last two years of secondary schooling represent the culmination of their hard work while for others they represent a struggle to redress their lack of effort in previous years. Some pupils at this stage grow in confidence and sense of purpose while others disengage and either drop out or merely bide their time. The two chapters, 'Confronting the world of work' and 'The reckoning', provide insight into the diverse and sometimes contradictory nature of the final stage of compulsory schooling.

During year 10 and year 11 pupils are expected to be closely focused on school in readiness for the final hurdles of coursework submissions and examinations – and then their attention is turned away from routine study to a quite different set of responsibilities and rhythms, and their status changes from that of 'pupil' to 'employee'. Although many pupils have had paid, part time jobs, work experience is, nevertheless, a significant moment for them; the majority anticipate taking on the role of 'worker' with excitement and, often, with some trepidation. In chapter 11, Day looks at the reactions of pupils to this initiation into employment, with its special rituals and demands. It is, for many pupils, a time for testing out some of their ideas about life after school – a time when curiosities and aspirations confront the realities of the working world. Work placements can have a powerful effect not only on students' plans for careers and further education and training, but also on their understanding of self and their attitudes towards school. Some pupils find a new relevance in learning as their goals become clearer; others find that their urge to leave school is quickened by their experience in the workplace. The chapter recognises that pupils often bring their own agenda to work experience and that their concerns may be at odds with those of the school, the employer and the government. The question remains as to whether the personal and often pragmatic expectations that pupils have of work experience can be acknowledged without losing the opportunity to extend pupils' grasp of the structure of organisations and their relationship to the country's economy.

Chapter 12 explores the final stage in pupils' school careers. The data from interviews conducted in the last two terms of compulsory secondary schooling suggest that this is a strange and sometimes poignant period for pupils. As they struggle to complete coursework and prepare for examinations their minds are also focused on the uncertainties and the new challenges which lie ahead of them. As they make their own personal reckonings of their experiences in school, a number of issues are identified which provide insight into the nature of the struggle that many young people have in making a success of their school careers. Many pupils regret past attitudes and behaviours; some manage to make the transition in good time – but others don't. The support of teachers and parents – and explicit statements of their trust in pupils to do well – are recognised as important factors in helping pupils to commit themselves to working for the examinations. Worryingly, perhaps, given the national concern to build commitments to the principle of life-long learning, the data reflect a picture of young people who are mainly working directly to short-term goals and who are not taking away with them a strong sense (which they may have had in the early years of secondary schooling) that the process of learning can be a positive and exciting experience in itself.

CHAPTER 11

Confronting the world of work

Julia Day

> *I think it was like a kid's phase [being a nursery nurse] you know. I like
> listened to what other people wanted to do and then I'd think, 'Oh, I'll
> do that' and just copying off people really. And now I haven't really
> got owt that I want to do. I like doing hairdressing, but like I've said, I
> don't really...But any job would really do me now. I just want a job for
> when I leave school else I'm not going to have anything...If I went to
> college then I wouldn't be getting no money in.*

A major criticism of the British educational system is that it has
consistently failed to meet the needs of industry. Employers, politicians
and media pundits decry the weakness of our educational system in not
equipping young people with the skills necessary to be useful employees.
The popular refrain has been: 'What do they teach them in schools these
days?' One response has been to bring the 'world of work' into the
educational domain through work experience programmes for pupils in
school. While the official aim of these schemes is to provide a general
introduction to the work environment, there has been some criticism (see
later) that they maintain sexual inequality and delimit aspirations. For
most pupils, however, they are an important transitional experience
where they learn, often, as much about themselves as about the structure
of the labour market and the workings of particular organisations within
it.

Work experience has become a key feature of the last 12 months of
compulsory schooling , holding a special significance for pupils, teachers
and policy-makers, although we know that each group has its own views
on its relevance and function. The extent of work experience programmes in the year 10 and year 11 curriculum has increased
dramatically since its first tentative appearance in the mid 1960s; it is
now an almost universal feature of secondary schools although there are
local variations in its organisation and implementation. Some work

experience schemes are linked with out-of-school organisations such as Project Trident while others are established independently by individual schools. Generally these schemes involve placement of pupils in a work environment for a two-week period (or, alternatively, but less commonly, for one day a week over a period of weeks); this limited exodus from the classroom is permitted under the legislation of the Education (Work Experience) Act of 1973. Government involvement in work experience schemes has been extensive, with various initiatives set in place over the past 20 years including the Technical and Vocational Education Initiative (TVEI), established in 1983 with the specified aim of incorporating 'learning about the world of work' into the final year curriculum. The TUC, the Schools Council and the CBI have also been actively involved and this wide base of interest has stimulated a dramatic expansion in work experience programmes; in 1975/76 only 7% of pupils were given access to work experience but by 1986 the figure had risen to 75% according to DES statistics (DES,1990), and in 1995 the percentage is probably considerably higher.

The researchers in the *Making Your Way Through Secondary School* study have conducted interviews with 80 pupils over a four-year period from 1991 to 1995; in the summer or autumn terms of 1994 the pupils from the three schools went out on their year 10 or year 11 placements and, following their placements, pupils were invited to comment on their work experience through questionnaires; we later followed up their comments in interviews. Through the data presented here we can listen to recent pupil reactions to work experience. The picture is a complex one but our data reveal some interesting aspects of how pupils approach their work experience, what personal gains they expect from it and how they adapt to the new role of employee.

Work experience – what's the point of it?

Work experience is quite a milestone in the final years of compulsory schooling and one which arouses a range of feelings and questions in pupils' minds. For many, apart from the usual paper rounds, baby-sitting and Saturday jobs, this will be the first taste of full-time adult work. While attitudes and emotions vary widely, few pupils are indifferent to the prospect of entering the working environment. Those who have not had part-time jobs already are presented with an opportunity to take on a completely new role and discover what it means to be a 'worker'. Typical comments of pupils about to go on work experience are these: 'You get experience of what it's like to work'; 'I want to see what it's like to work'; '[You learn] what it's actually like to be in the working atmosphere'.

There is also a growing sense of unease amongst pupils as they near the end of compulsory schooling and have to confront the fact that a major decision-point in their lives is approaching. The familiar structures of school life – days segmented into short chunks of time, school bells, timetables, the web of rules and rituals – experienced for the past 12 years are about to stop. For those who have no definite career plans the future can be a daunting prospect and work experience takes on special relevance as an important opportunity to come up with some ideas – as one pupil said, in a remark typical of many: 'I want to know what I want to do. I don't know what I want to do when I leave school'. In the shorter term, some pupils want to use work experience to help them decide whether or not to go into further education, hoping that somehow the short placement will tip the balance in their decision-making – and sometimes it does! Work placements may lead to a rejection of further education if the pupil finds full-time work attractive or they may encourage pupils to seek further training and qualifications to meet the requirements of the jobs they now have in mind.

For those who do have some idea of what they would like to do as a career, work experience is an opportunity for clarification. It offers a trial run without a binding commitment, a test not only of what the work involves but also of the pupils' abilities and propensities. For many pupils this is a crucial stage as their future plans begin to crystallise through sampling adult working roles; in this confrontation with 'reality' they learn some aspects of a particular job and, perhaps more importantly, they acquire a sense of themselves as workers. Dipping a toe in the water is important: 'I wanted to be a hairdresser when I left school but it'll just make me think about it, see if it's any good' (Y11,F); 'If I like it I think that's what I'd like to do, like work in a building society or something like that, like clerical work and all that' (Y10,M).

Among those who have made up their minds and feel committed to their plans, some may find that it is not possible to obtain a placement in their chosen field. For many aspiring to professional careers there can be difficulty in finding employers willing to take on a 15 or 16 year old; the nature of the work involved often prevents the non-qualified from taking an active role. The approach to a placement outside the chosen career is, understandably, less enthusiastic: 'It might not be a waste of time, it may be worthwhile if you want a job like that...but I want to work with animals so it would be a waste of time for me' (Y10,M). Even so, the chance to try something different is appreciated by some pupils who have been given placements outside their own ambitions; as one pupil said, 'I don't think it's going to be right useful because I want to be a singer as a career...but if it's somat that I enjoy at least I can fall back on that. Like, if I've tried it out and I like it I can fall back on that idea, can't I?' (Y10,F).

Finding suitable placements is a problem in many areas but the way in which pupils approach their work experience is, to some extent, coloured by their understanding of why they end up with a particular placement. In one school involved in our project, each pupil makes three suggestions which are then sent to the Trident Office whose staff identify the placements. Some are lucky and get their first choice, others end up in a placement that was not on their list. The other two schools arrange placements independently; in one, the pupils are actively encouraged to make their own arrangements if possible, with the support and guidance of a member of the teaching staff. The other school provides a list of local employers offering places but pupils can negotiate a placement for themselves if they wish. While using family networks gives easier access to placements, this approach may serve to maintain class distinctions; professional families can offer access to higher status placements which working-class pupils find difficult to obtain. Finding a range of placements can be very difficult in some areas and pupils, who do not always understand the constraints, may be disappointed, fearing that the placement is a 'palming off': 'They're probably just going to send us to Sainsbury's or something'. Some see the selection of placements as more evaluative than it usually is in practice and they think that the slot chosen for them reflects teachers' opinions of their personality or abilities:

> Well if we want to do something in construction then if we're a good enough pupil they might try and get us with a firm that has something to do with construction...if you're good enough and if the teachers think you're good enough then they might be able to send you to a firm that, you know, deals in that area you want to have a job in. (Y10,M)

Problems can arise when pupils are allowed to approach employers direct. One pupil described, with great disappointment, how she had written 20 letters to employers and had been rejected by every one. With so many hopes and decisions resting on work experience, the type of placement offered and its allocation is an issue requiring very careful consideration. Pupils wishing to work with a parent or in the family firm were often coerced into alternative placements and they did not always understand the logic of the school in frustrating their wishes, especially in cases where they expected to be employed by their parent later on: 'Like on us Tridents I think like we should be allowed to work with our parents because I think where parents have their own businesses...I work with my dad [at weekends] anyway' (Y10,M). Understanding something of the way the world of business and industry works was not on this young person's agenda. In the face of the uncertain or unknown, pupils may, understandably, find security in following in the family footsteps: 'My brother worked in a warehouse in Marks and Spencers, so anything like that...' (Y10,M); 'Mum, she went to a shoe shop like on her Trident and she said she enjoyed it so I thought I'll put it down' (Y10,F). Such comments reveal the extent to which pupils look to their families to provide a pattern for adult life. Although work experience may be seen by schools as a means of opening up alternatives, clearly this aspiration is, to some extent, being resisted by pupils. The purposes they bring to work experience are often very much their own.

A minority of pupils are actually pinning their hopes on work experience leading to a job – it is a potential first step into the job market. This expectation is sometimes fulfilled; the data gathered in this project show a small number of full-time and part-time job offers arising from work experience placements. For the majority of pupils, though, the anticipated gains from work experience are broader and of a more personal nature. When asked what they consider is the point of work experience, many pupils refer to learning how to adapt to the new social environment of the workplace. The role of employee is a new one to most of them and one which carries great significance for the pupils themselves and in the wider society, conferring social status and material wealth.

At the same time, the seriousness of being a 'worker' can cause pupils anxiety. Many of those about to undertake work experience placements distinguish the social aspects of the job as being the most important. And for some, even the social side of work can be a source of anxiety as they face novel circumstances and settings. For pupils, learning to cope in these new surroundings is an important element of work experience schemes:

> If I was going somewhere where I knew somebody who worked there I might be a little bit more at ease because I could think 'Oh well, if I get anything wrong they can show me how to do it.' But if I had to go somewhere where I didn't know anybody it would be like 'Oh my, oh dear' and I wouldn't know what to do. (Y10,F)

> I feel right little with all the people there...and I'm scared of doing something wrong. (Y10,M)

Another focus of anxiety is the practical arrangements, such as getting up, wearing the appropriate clothes and travelling to and from the workplace. Briefing sessions prior to the work placement are helpful in allaying some of these concerns but many pupils still worry about how they will cope with the everyday matters:

> I don't want to work in that [placement in a restaurant]...You've got to wear like a uniform or somat where you've got to wear a skirt because I haven't got a skirt. I don't like wearing skirts. (Y10,F)

> I don't want somat too far away though because I don't like travelling. (Y10,F)

Generally, pupils were not looking to work experience for a grounding in the basic skills specific to their placement; a few expressed hopes of learning the ropes of the type of work involved but they recognised that the limited time available allowed little more than a 'taster' of the job. No one expected to acquire sufficient skills during the short period of the placement to enable them to step directly into that kind of work when they left school but there were some who saw the experience as being useful in introducing them to techniques of applying for jobs and job-hunting skills.

As we have seen, pupils approach their work experience with their own personal agenda, anxieties and expectations. For almost all pupils this landmark in the final year of compulsory schooling presents a challenge and an opportunity and their responses are often surprising to themselves and also to their teachers and parents. This chapter so far has suggested something of their aims and anxieties, their hopes and their excitement prior to their placement, but does reality match up to the expectations?

The experience of work: 'So that's what it's all about'

Our interview and questionnaire data give an intriguing picture of the range of pupils' responses to work experience programmes. While there are, of course, variations in what pupils take away with them from their work experience, very few have not found the experience valuable in some way. Some refer explicitly to work experience leading to changes in thoughts about their future and in attitudes to school work. Many are surprised by what they find in the world of work, and by their own reactions. There is a clear sense of re-evaluation in the comments made by our pupils in terms of their own identity, and a reassessment of their future place in the world outside the school gates. In assessing their work placements pupils tend to put a greater emphasis on the social aspects of work and on self-discovery than on the practical or structural aspects of the work. Many stress the impact the experience has had on their confidence and self-awareness. These extracts from interviews and questionnaire responses illustrate the range of pupil reactions to, and interpretations of, 'being a worker':

> I have learnt from work experience that you have to stick up for yourself and that if you don't like how someone is treating you, you should say so and not keep quiet about it. (Y11,F)

> I enjoyed that work experience fortnight, definitely. And I've been, had more confidence in myself, talking in PSE and stuff like that. I enjoy more lessons now. I'm more open. (Y11,M)

> I learned that people don't just go on the appearance of you but from your working ability. (Y11,M)

> It got me a bit more confident because I'm a bit quiet most of the time but I'm a bit bolder now. (Y11,M)

> I learned that I had a lot of patience in me and it was harder than I thought. (Y11,F)

The personal re-evaluation brought about through work experience also extends to job plans and attitudes towards further education. For those using work experience to clarify what they want to do after compulsory education, the de-briefing phase is a crucial time, presenting an opportunity to readjust ideas in the light of firsthand experience and information. For some the change will be radical, as one option is closed down in favour of another: 'I have changed my decision from a solicitor to a pharmacist because I enjoyed working in the chemist' (Y11,F); 'Work experience has changed my mind because before I wanted to be a journalist but now I'm more interested in administration work' (Y11,M).

The process can be a disturbing one as long-cherished notions crumble following this confrontation with adult work: 'I find out every single bit what you've got to do, you know, and found out that I can't do this work. If I want to I still can if I try my best, but I think it's very hard for me' (Y10,F). Another pupil abandoned her plans to be a primary teacher following a placement in a primary classroom: 'I suppose it sort of made me decide that I don't ever want to be a teacher. I mean I wouldn't mind working with children but I just...I wouldn't like to go through that every day!' (Y10,F). Future plans are often readjusted as a result of work experience whether the placement itself was viewed positively or not, as other studies confirm (for example, Varlaam, 1984; Shilling, 1987). Placements which have not been successful in pupils' eyes colour their views of working life but may serve to re-motivate them to try and avoid this kind of work in the future. One pupil, after a strenuous manual labour placement with a local building firm declared; 'It teaches you to work hard at school so you can get...[qualifications and have]...a nice easy office job or something' (Y10,M).

In more general terms, pupils discover what it means to be an employee. The world of work is encountered at first hand and challenges their preconceptions about the working environment. Pupils' comments often centre on the mundane nature of the work that they have undertaken: 'It was more boring than I expected. Forever being on your feet and the day seems to drag on' (Y11,F); 'I was surprised that work is not as hard as people make out; it is just boring and repetitive' (Y11,M); 'I learnt that I wasn't made for work!' (Y11,M). It is interesting to see how pupils compare school work with this experience: 'I found it harder [than school] and more tiring, a bit boring. No chance to socialise...' (Y11,F). The range of tasks which work experience placements can offer in the span of one or two weeks is limited and the impression created by the experience is often quite a distorted one. And yet an employer striving to offer an interesting variety of tasks to the pupil may give an unrealistic impression of the job, glossing over the mundane and repetitive aspects often involved.

One aspect pupils particularly enjoyed and valued was being given the opportunity to show their own initiative; they appreciated being trusted and given responsibility:

> I was left alone to put up a Hallowe'en display. I enjoyed this because I had independence and I could decide where everything went. (Y11,F)

> Oh, I did all sorts. I did using computers, different sorts of filing, photocopying...and I did that, you know, tax invoices and stuff, sorting them out and stuff, like. Every day it was a different task, and people were being helpful if you needed anything but they wouldn't just tell you what; they would say come and show you how to do it and when we're sure you can do it then we leave it to you. (Y10,M)

Being given independence and an interesting range of tasks was fundamental to successful placements; as Chris Shilling reported from his earlier study (1987, p. 418), the positive responses made by pupils about their placements 'were characterised by a labour process providing what they regarded as variety and/or autonomy'.

Criticisms about work experience placements often centred on pupils not being given the chance to show initiative or take responsibility. Unpopular placements were characterised as those where pupils were given no chance to become involved in the 'real' work but were expected to carry out simple service tasks like coffee-making and shelf-filling. This girl describes the type of work she experienced in a retirement home:

> Well, all skivvy jobs really. I had to feed them in the mornings and then tidy up dining room after. Then making all the beds...well, there weren't really a lot for me to do. I were stood around most of the time. (Y10,F)

Another girl found the placement she had chosen with a community theatre group was far less glamorous than she had imagined:

> It was boring really. They just made me deliver over 10,000 leaflets during the two weeks and that's really all I did. Just walking all over the place delivering leaflets, by foot, when they've all got cars. (Y10,F)

Clearly these difficulties arise from the pressure on the placements; some employers are unable or unwilling to make 'special' arrangements for pupils and, because obtaining sufficient placements is often a problem, schools cannot screen out all the employers who provide unchallenging placements. Another issue pupils raised was the length and number of work placements offered. Some felt placements were too short while others felt that they would have liked to try more than one type of job:

> Because I found that it was like an insight into what goes on but seeing as you can't really compare it with anything else. I mean if you had another week, choose something else and you could say 'Oh well, I preferred this or whatever'. You don't know how much of what went on was like, would be the same anyway. (Y10,M)

The National Curriculum Council guidelines (NCC,1990) urged schools to broaden work-related programmes and thread them through the five or more years of secondary schooling, but at the moment coursework and examination pressures in years 10 and 11 make it difficult for teachers to give more time to work experience itself unless it is a necessary element in the content of a particular course of study.

Back to school

Finally, we look at how the pupils respond to school on their return from work experience. Some pupils refer to the effect of work experience on their self-confidence in school and on their attitude to school, particularly as an incentive to work harder, whether the actual placement was viewed positively or not:

> What kind of things did you learn, do you think?

> Well the best thing is the atmosphere, what it is actually like to be in the working atmosphere. It's sort of made me think about working harder at school as well. (Y10,M)

The new environment of work has a marked effect on some pupils which can be carried back into the classroom. One teacher, who had responsibility for supervising work experience placements, commented on the effects work experience had on some pupils' attitudes to school:

This past few weeks [name] has settled down very well and there is a more mature side of her coming out. She did her work experience at a primary school, one of our feeder primary schools, and she did very well. They were very pleased with her and I think the responsibility of working with younger children...helped her realise that when she gets out into the big wide world she'll have to settle down a bit.

He did extremely well; they were very impressed with him. He is very ambitious and he realises now that he needs to settle down and listen. I think he is settling down...particularly when we were preparing for work experience; he got his head down and got on with it.

Seeing their pupils in a new context also gave teachers a better understanding of them and their needs at this important, transitional phase of their school career. Another teacher was surprised and delighted by the changed attitudes he noted in most of his pupils as he observed them during their work experience fortnight, particularly one young man who had shown signs of disaffection in school:

[Name] was great! I mean he was knackered. When I went to see him he had a petrol tank on his back and strimmer on the front and he got there on time at six o'clock in the morning, leaving home at five am, having to go to bed [in the afternoon] to be fit for the following morning. So he's making good decisions about his future, you know.

Seeing a different side of pupils helped teachers to adjust their images of some pupils and this may have opened up the possibility of a different kind of relationship during the last phase of the year 10 and 11 work.

The effects were not universally positive, however. For some, the experience deepened their disaffection with school, as in this case where a pupil found a placement working in the same factory as his father. A teacher comments:

He is guaranteed this job at the end of the school year so he is actually working there on Saturdays as well and is not bothered about school anymore. He's just not interested. He's just coming in, doing his bit and going home and even when I spoke to him the other day about filling in his Personal Statement for his ROA he said 'Oh, it doesn't matter. I've got a job anyway'.

This issue has been identified in the literature on work experience as central to the dilemma created when the worlds of education and employment meet. Brown (1987, p. 12) offers a warning: 'Unless they perceive a clear relationship between the products of 'making an effort' in school and rewards in the labour market...pupils will see little point in bothering to comply because their interest in much of what is taught them is limited to those 'practical' subjects which are believed to have some relevance and interest for them' (see also chapter 6). Work experience can lead to a rejection, therefore, of the formal curriculum as some pupils feel that they know where they are heading, that they already have the limited range of specific skills required for their chosen job and that school has nothing more to offer them.

Conclusion

Through listening to our pupils talking about work experience we can appreciate the degree of importance many of them attach to it. But in the light of their comments we must carefully evaluate the quality of experience being offered to them. We need to look closely at the potential of work experience as part of the final year curriculum, acknowledging the strong personal influence that placements can have on pupils. Some pupils returned from their work experience with negative or distorted impressions of the workplace. Few had been given the chance to explore new ideas and abilities in the placements they were offered. The work experience often appeared to be part of a delimiting strategy, as Brown (1987, p. 8) pointed out: 'British research has consistently found that the school has been very successful in regulating the ambition of school leavers so that they fit the available opportunities in the labour market'.

On the question of how work experience programmes should be conducted there are a number of recommendations for practice in schools. One of the primary considerations in arranging placements must be to extend pupils' aspirations. While every attempt should be made to meet pupils' own interests and preferences they could be encouraged to broaden the scope of their interests, and if time *can* be found (and if the organisational arrangements can be managed) then more than one placement (ideally offering a contract of some kind) might be tried. In particular, there should be a challenge to class and gender stereotyping; work experience placements are a genuine opportunity to break out of the familiar scenario of 'hairdressing for girls' and 'car maintenance for boys', but there was little evidence of these moulds being broken, despite strong commitments in the schools to equality of opportunity and the challenging of gender work stereotypes. (We recognise, of course, that to a large extent choice is constrained by the structure of opportunities locally available.) This raises the question of whose agenda holds the priority. Clearly, pupils have their own purposes in mind as they approach work experience and, as we have seen, these are often different from those of schools and policy-makers. The National Curriculum puts considerable emphasis on work experience as a means of developing a stronger understanding of the nature and structure of employment:

Work observation and experience should be part of a planned programme of activities designed to relate aspects of the curriculum to working life. Preparation and follow-up are essential if effective links with other parts of the curriculum are to be made. Pupils involved in placements should be encouraged to explore, as a group, how their experiences help them learn about the nature of work, industry and the local economy.

(NCC, 1990, p. 6)

Many young people are looking to work experience to provide them with directions for their own futures and reactions are often very personal and even job specific. There is a need to prepare for (see Wallace, 1985) and evaluate work experience more thoroughly in the light of the pupils' agenda. We may need to move away from the common view that 'the experience is the thing' but at the same time we need to respect the nature of young people's concerns at this important stage in their transition from pupil to worker; and if we work only to the agenda set by pupils then we lose the opportunity to challenge their assumptions about work. That is the nature of the dilemma.

References

Brown, P. (1987) 'Schooling for inequality? Ordinary kids in school and the labour market', in P. Brown and D. N. Ashton (1987) *Education, Unemployment and Labour Markets*. Lewes: The Falmer Press.

HMI (1990) *Work Experience and Work Shadowing: Some Aspects of Good Practice*. London: DES.

National Curriculum Council (1990) *Curriculum Guidance 4: Education for Economic and Industrial Understanding*. London: NCC.

Shilling, C. (1987) 'Work experience as contradictory practice'. *British Journal of Sociology of Education*, **8**, 4, 407–423.

Varlaam, C. (ed.) (1984) *Rethinking Transition: Educational Innovation and the Transition to Adult Life*. Lewes: The Falmer Press.

Wallace, R. G. (1985) *Introducing Technical and Vocational Education*. London: Macmillan Educational.

CHAPTER 12

The reckoning

Julia Day

...at beginning of fifth year it didn't really matter and then one day it were like somat just came and hit me over the head and said, wake up. And like I realised that I've got to do somat. And like before I didn't...I didn't think it were going to be owt like this. I mean now it doesn't feel like I'm going to be leaving school in a month [or two]...I keep thinking that it's going to come to that day and I'm still going to school anyway weeks after, but I'm not.

(A year 11 pupil)

Students have a right to expect that the school will make unabated efforts to provide them with the basic skills necessary for living an autonomous life in our society.

(Stenhouse, 1975)

The pupils involved in the *Making Your Way Through Secondary School* study (see chapter 1) have now reached their final term in compulsory education and are preparing for their GCSEs. While revising for examinations and finalising coursework take up much of their energies, they are also thinking about this important crossroads in their lives. They are looking ahead to their futures with mixed feelings of anxiety and confidence, excitement and disquiet as they confront the prospect of leaving school and taking their first steps on new paths which, mostly, they have chosen for themselves. But, like Janus, some are also looking back and taking stock of their past five years in secondary school, reflecting on what it is has meant to them and where it will enable them to go. As these year 11 pupils ready themselves to take on new roles as workers, as apprentices or as college or sixth form pupils, they are also taking a retrospective view of their role as pupils and their comments offer some valuable insights through which we may analyse the influences which have shaped their individual school careers. In examining educational experiences from this 'consumer perspective' we can begin to draw out the threads which have patterned children's learning experiences. Throughout this book, pupils' voices are taken as a starting point from which to think about ways of improving schools and here we listen to pupils at the end of their school careers evaluating their educational experiences, discussing plans for the future and asking themselves if their schooling has prepared them for autonomous lives as adults in the world beyond the school gates.

It was in the spring term of 1995 that the pupils were last invited to talk about where they were up to. Work experience was five months or more behind them and they were now preparing for their examinations and trying to formulate plans for the next stage of their lives. Some were already applying for jobs and post-16 courses, others had yet to decide what to do and where to go. In this time of turmoil and pressure they perceived their moment of leaving school as unsettling. Two themes dominated pupils' accounts of their schooling and, rather like the warp and weft, gave structure to the pattern of learning experiences of individual pupils. One was their attitude towards learning and school; they saw how their attitudes had changed and developed as they moved through the formal structures of secondary school life. The other was the influence of relationships, both within school and outside, on their learning.

Attitudes towards learning and school

'It's gone so fast!' was a common cry; the pupils saw the past five years as a series of rapid transitions, beginning with the confusion and excitement of joining the school in year 7 through to the 'serious graft' of years 10 and 11. Pupils often remarked that their final two years required them to make a radical shift into a higher gear which demanded consistent effort in school work if rewards were to be gained. With future plans at stake, learning was now a matter of 'playing for real'. As one girl put it:

> I just took it all as a game at first and I wish now that I knew what I know now and then I could have tried harder, but can't turn back time so I'm just going to have to try and do my hardest now. (Y11,F)

Many pupils felt that no one had forewarned them and that they were ill-equipped for this new situation. They looked back upon the earlier years, particularly 7 and 8, as being 'fun' times and now found themselves engaged in something altogether more serious which might affect them for the rest of their lives. The responses to this realisation were varied, but in many cases regret was the initial reaction. The comments of these pupils were echoed by others – mainly but not exclusively male:

> A lot of regrets. Looking back at this year I've got, not this year but last year, especially last year in the fourth year, if I'd just started working at the start of the fourth year and carried on. You don't have to work hard but you just have to work consistently and you'd be able to pass most of your grades. It's a bit late now but I suppose better late than never. (Y11,M)

> When I think back I think I would have liked, you know, to start again because I realise now that there's been so much time that I've wasted. Like we say to each other, 'Oh better start working', [then] something trivial would always crop up and that would be our main priority. But now we realise that every minute could have been useful so we've got to like put ourselves in for extra work now. But like I say if I'd worked constantly all the way through, not major league, but put some time in, I think I could be doing better than I am now. (Y11,M)

> I wish I'd got down and got my work done and that. Everybody were going on about Trident and all that and going on about all the exams coming up and that. I were lost. Like other people like getting on ahead of me and like I were looking back and thinking why shouldn't I be up there? (Y11,M)

Many of those who had previously been disruptive in class found themselves regretting their past behaviour and their lack of self-control – having understood, somewhat belatedly, the implications of their actions:

> I think trouble were with me when I come to school I messed about from day one so people like got me as a mess abouter from day one so like if I didn't mess about, 'Oh you're boring!' And so I think I've got to keep my name, haven't I? Best mess about. And I think I wish I'd not messed about when I first come. (Y11,F)

> I think I used to mess around quite a lot because I didn't really think. But it's too late now, isn't it? (Y11,M)

> I shouldn't have been so naughty. Always naughty. (Y11,M)

Those who were not reforming their classroom behaviour at this late stage found themselves alienated from their friends, who had adopted a different attitude towards them. These two pupils, who were formerly disruptive in class, expressed their current disapproval of the antics of non-conforming pupils:

> They'd rather just sit there and mess about. You have to forget about them. They don't think we've only got a month left at school. So it's rest of us life, isn't it, we're talking about. (Y11,M)

> We used to be a big group together and now we've like split up into two segments. Those who are hard core, they just want to doss all the time, and there's others who can't afford to doss all the time. (Y11,M)

As the quotations suggest, the small minority who haven't managed the transition and who are still attending school are increasingly likely, at this stage, to be rejected by their peers. No longer the class jesters, they are more likely to be seen as the class nuisances – still playing the same old games that their peers no longer find so amusing, still baiting the ill-fated supply teachers: 'Well, like we'll see what teacher we've got first, like if he's a strict one we'll do some work. But if it's like a supply teacher we test them, you know I mean? See how far we can go with them' (Y11,M).

How can we account for these changing attitudes to work, particularly in year 11? Clearly, the majority of pupils at this stage are spurred on by the rewards they see attached to examination success, even those, as we have noted, whose attentions were, in the past, distracted by the social side of school life. The level of their commitment is probably affected by the extent to which they believe their endeavours will pay off; those who feel they have little or no chance of attaining acceptable grades have either dropped out of the system altogether or continue to attend, taking the social side of schooling as their rationale for being there. A teacher described the attitude of one of the year 11 pupils:

> He has gone down the slippery slope and is beyond retrieval, I think. He's given up on his schoolwork. He's not entered for some exams and literally has given up now. He's just biding his time 'til he leaves and he's made that plain. He's as destructive as he can be in lessons.

The pupil concerned failed to hand in his coursework for some subjects and, realising that he had little chance of success in other GCSEs, spoke of his regret, explaining that 'sometimes I get carried away with messing around'.

Pupils in this position, whose experiences are largely of failure and disappointment, are often caught up in a vicious circle where motivation to learn is dependent on competitive measures of achievement. As Carole Ames (1986, p. 236) has said, 'Students experience success and failure in the context of certain learning goals, evaluational systems and so forth, and these contextual factors serve to shape students' motivation and opportunities to become involved in their own learning'. But while some year 11 pupils are acknowledging feelings of anxiety and regret, others are finding that the context of *significant* assessment is a key to engagement with learning and many claim to be enjoying the challenges of working towards a clearly defined goal. In earlier years there was often a dismissive attitude towards school work, which pupils did not see as important and often did not experience as either relevant or coherent. Now, however, their GCSE studies have given shape and a sense of seriousness to their work:

> It doesn't matter like what you've learned in first, second or third [years]. It's like end of fourth and beginning of fifth that you start doing stuff that counts and its got nowt to do with first, second or third...Might just as well have just come fourth and fifth and have done with it. (Y11,M)

> Like in first and second and third year it were just like, weren't really much you could do which would alter anything now. (Y11,F)

Conversely, for some highly-motivated year 11 pupils who have been committed to learning throughout their school careers, the pressures of GCSE work can become too heavy; some begin to doubt their competence or are striving too hard, as this teacher says of one of them:

> She is very academically able, very aspiring in her own way, wants to achieve well. She went through quite a lot of anxiety when her elder brother got all As at GCSEs and has gone on to do A levels and is reported to be doing very well...She went through a really turbulent time when she felt she could never be as good as him. And in her parents' eyes, they were always comparing him, and so on.

This contrasts with the experience of one male pupil in the same school who, in previous years, had failed to achieve the level of attainment his teachers felt he was capable of because of his 'attitude' towards school work. Apparently the focus on assessment and the realisation that teachers and family really *did* think he could do well had reversed his attitude towards school work and helped to build up his self-esteem:

> [I] just feel more confident, a lot more confident. In year 10 I were working quite hard and I weren't really that confident. You tend not to do so good but then, that parents' evening, mum says you're going to have to try your best now because it being the last year. She says, teachers say you *can* pass them all if you try. So it just made me feel more confident and my work seems better. So I can get my good grades at GCSEs and then I can mess about then when I've finished them. (Y11,M)

Those who have made up their minds about the directions they will take, and know what they must achieve in order to realise these ambitions, are ready to lay aside distractions and adopt a more conscientious attitude towards their work. The pupils quoted below have sorted out their plans for the future and are aware of the levels of achievement that they must reach to attain their goals:

> Year 11 is very important to me because of the GCSEs. It is important because I am hoping I will get good grades and move on to college to do an art and design course or leisure and recreation. (Y11,M)

> I'll work for the GCSEs because I need that. Because if not it's going to take me even longer to be an art therapist, I need at least five A to C GCSEs. (Y11,F)

Others pupils, although uncertain of the direction they will take at the end of year 11, still attach great importance to achieving good grades, either to give them a better chance of success in the job market or to open doors into further education. There is a widespread acknowledgement that 'respectable' grades are the crux of the matter, as another research study (Nash, 1995) recently concluded:

> In spite of the rhetoric surrounding GCSEs as an examination for all, the Grade C cliff still exists, not only in the minds of the students but embedded in the system. If you reach the top of the cliff then a whole new landscape opens up. You can choose to do A levels or advanced GNVQ or you can elect, as some did, to do an intermediate GNVQ and consolidate your position. Less than Grade C and you are back at the bottom of the cliff and must start to climb again.

In discussing their hopes for the future many pupils began their comments with 'If I get the grades...', particularly those whose aim was to continue into further education. Uncertainty about what to do if they did not achieve these grades was a major source of anxiety. Of the pupils who took part in the spring term interviews about 14% still had no clear plans for what to do after leaving school, 46% were applying for further education or training, and 30% said that they wanted to go straight into a job and were looking for work (the figures offer only a rough, snap-shot picture of what is a fluid situation). Most pupils were aware of the local job market situation and were worried about unemployment and competition for jobs. Their responses were realistic: 'The unemployment these days! I suppose that is a kind of incentive really. Have to get the best qualifications you can' (Y11,M). On the other hand, for those whose families have direct experience of long-term unemployment, messages about qualifications being the passport to jobs can sound hollow.

Although motivation engendered by the need for qualifications and planning for the future may exert a powerful influence on some pupils, others still fail to find a meaning and purpose for applying themselves to their school work because they do not see its relevance to their own personal needs. The following pupils were seen as underachieving in their final year and they do not see a lack of good grades as having any serious effect on their plans for the future:

> [Year 11] is rubbish! All these deadlines and all the work. [I'm going to] join the army, I've always fancied it...If I just went in as ordinary without no things [i.e. qualifications] I'd be like bottom of list and rank and everything. [But] I want to just get in and get a job and get some money. (Y11,M)

> When I've left school, I'm getting myself down to it...probably construction, building and that. I don't think it means going to college.

Probably needs training but I don't think I'll have to do it because my mate's dad, he owns like a roofing company so if I can get set on with him it's all right. Get to know all the tricks of the trade and that, see all the skills what they do, and if anybody asks me, I can jump in. (Y11,M)

We were surprised to find so many young people who were opting for the (possibly short-term) security of being taken on by family or friends of family but the local context explains the logic of their decision.

An underlying issue which emerges from the varied responses to the future is the extent to which pupils believe that the process of learning is under their 'ownership'. By 'ownership' we mean the balance of freedom and control pupils experience as they confront decision points in relation to their lives and learning. From the vantage point of year 11 some pupils feel they have acquired a greater responsibility for determining their commitment to school work and for shaping the contours of their lives beyond compulsory schooling; they have exercised some choice in the subjects they work hard at, they are encouraged to organise their pattern of study themselves and they see the end results as being directly beneficial. 'Its down to me,' is a sentiment commonly expressed by this year group. Learning 'for fun' is an experience associated with the early years of secondary school which most pupils choose to reject in favour of a 'serious' concentration on coursework and examinations in years 10 and 11. But it was striking, however, that so few acknowledged any purposes for learning *beyond* attaining the grades (see also chapter 6). Many at this stage spoke of certain subjects being 'useless' because they felt they would not be required for their future employment: 'I know for most jobs you've got to have maths and English so I'm trying to do well in them but like I'm just forgetting the lessons...like French and Art and PE. I don't need them for a job not unless I want to be an artist or gymnast' (Y11,F). If pupils are not seeing the purpose of learning for its own sake, or even for longer term pay-offs, this may explain why the drop out rate from further education courses has, according to official inspections (Nash, 1995), recently risen to nearly 25%: pupils are quick to turn to what they see as more immediately meaningful or lucrative alternatives to education.

Family influences on learning

There were many references in the interviews to the influence of relationships with parents, and pupils often related aspects of their family life to their work in school, particularly during the final two years. The evidence suggests that parents were, on the whole, very supportive and were trying to give encouragement, advice and guidance by whatever means they could – for example, by helping with revision, laying down rules for working before socialising, discussing plans and even simply 'keeping quiet'. Occasionally parents' aspirations created problems and added to the burdens of stress experienced by individual pupils, particularly during year 11. However, it was interesting to note the direct and positive impact parents could have on those who had previously not taken their school work seriously. The views of parents sometimes led to surprising reactions:

> Dad thinks I'm a waster, says because I've messed about all the way through school and got bad reports and stuff...so I just want to prove them wrong, that I can be brainy if I want to be. Prove them wrong! (Y11,F)

One potential non-attender (Y11,M) took heed of the short, sharp advice of his mother: 'Me Mum says, "Go or die"' – and her words seemed to be having a positive impact! Some pupils were less fortunate; problems arising from their family circumstances hampered their chances of success in school in various ways. One girl spoke of her difficult home life and its effects upon her schooling, which finally led to her dropping out of school before the GCSE examinations:

> This year I have been attending school less and less. First it started because I couldn't cope with the work. Then I didn't come because I got kicked out of my house and I had no money to come to school. (Y11,F)

It was apparent from our data that there were a number of pupils who were no longer coming to school on a regular basis. The cohort included a number of unofficial 'early leavers' who had dropped out of school during the last two terms in order to take up job opportunities offered by relatives. This was particularly so in construction trades which tend to have seasonal employment patterns and this perhaps explains the departure of some young male pupils from the classroom in the late spring. Most of these non-attenders saw little point in attempting GCSEs; they preferred to be out in the adult world, earning money and 'getting on with it'. The attractions of working for a parent are explained by this young man:

> I've been offered a job working for my dad because he owns his own business. He's a car valeter so I thought I'd take that up. You don't feel the hassles of interviews and well, I've been working for quite a while now so I don't need training. (Y11,M)

In one case we found that a pupil's awareness of job shortages locally had led him to go out at the start of the summer term – a few weeks before taking his exams, in which his teachers expected him to get above-average grades. Teachers had sent messages to and visited his parents but the pupil could not balance the value of 'paper qualifications' against the prospect of securing a job before the other members of his year group left school a few weeks later. Many parents, at this stage of their son's or daughter's maturity, are uncertain how to exert influence and can only say something like: 'It's their life. They'll do what they want to do'.

Teacher influences on learning

Relationships at school are also an important influence affecting pupils' attitudes to their learning and it is apparent from our data that many pupils valued the changed pupil–teacher relationships associated with year 11 status. Teachers were felt to be more friendly and approachable than in the past and some pupils observed that this gave them a more positive attitude towards learning itself: 'It has helped me get more out of my lessons knowing that my teacher will treat me with respect' (Y11,M). Support and advice from teachers during the stressful period of coursework deadlines and revision were also appreciated: 'Like teachers treat you more different because they know you've got coursework and like do allow you a few days if they know you've got coursework from other lessons' (Y11,F). Some pupils, however, felt that their relationships with teachers lay at the root of their disaffection with school. Several pupils associated the problems they had in their relationships with teachers to the institutional habit of 'image-fixing': they felt individual teachers had built up an image of them from which they could not escape. One pupil gave an account of the problems he faced in trying to change his image and avoid further suspensions while struggling to improve his chances of success in the GCSEs: 'You see in this school, because I'm so big, they always try and do me for bullying, but I don't...They think I go round picking everyone up and I don't. You can't put one thing out of place or you're there, out!' (Y11,M).

On the other hand, some who had often been the leaders of disruptive activities in class felt that their achievement in school would have been greater if the school had been more 'strict':

> I wish...cause with it being like this year about league tables, getting all these passes and that, because [that] school's a lot stricter than ours...they're the ones that get most passes at the end of the school year and I think ours were the last one...Well, if this school were more strict then we'd get more work done but because they let slip sometimes and let people mess about you just think, 'Oh, just stuff it! I'll just mess about' and so you don't get your work done. (Y11,F)

Several passages in the interviews underline the very real concern pupils have about small-scale classroom disruption. A recent OFSTED conference report (1995) concerning school improvement schemes in urban areas confirmed the value of an approach which sought to involve young people more in helping to find solutions to classroom problems:

> Every school has sought to address the broader issues of school climate and, particularly, the management of behaviour. Here again, it has been the practice to involve the young people as widely as possible in the process. It is intended that involving the pupils in this way encourages positive pupil/teacher relationships built on mutual support and trust. (p.10)

While a whole-school approach to strengthening pupils' commitment to learning is valuable there is also an opportunity for the teacher as an individual to make a difference. One pupil gave his advice on what makes a good teacher (see also chapter 3):

> I'd stand my ground. I'd let them [the pupils] go so far, then I'd stand my ground. I'd be like a multi-personality. Be a laugh when you need to be a laugh and be serious when you need to be serious. But if anything serious [i.e. an incident] come out like that, I'd listen to both sides of the story and if I didn't agree with any of them I'd get them both out. You can't lean on to one and the other, not one take the punch and the other not. (Y11,M)

Summary

From the year 10 and year 11 interviews a picture has emerged which offers some guidance for improving aspects of schooling that affect young people's learning. It seems that motivation can be enhanced through the focusing-power of national assessment, which underlines the seriousness of attainment: the rewards are clearly understood by pupils ('I need to get decent grades because I want a decent job', Y10,M). However, it doesn't work like that for all pupils; those who think, for whatever reason, that they have very little chance of success in examinations and coursework may distance themselves further from their learning. Academic success has traditionally been prioritised in our system of education; those whose abilities are not conventionally 'academic' may be disadvantaged by the paraphernalia, conditions and pressures of the assessment system as it currently stands. As David Hargreaves (1982, p.56) pointed out, 'The hidden curriculum message is clear: only knowledge, skills and abilities that can be readily measured, especially in a written text, are to be treated as *really* valuable'. This is now widely recognised. What is needed – and the new system of vocationally-oriented courses and qualifications is being heralded by many teachers with optimism – is a network of opportunities which will encourage all pupils to recognise and develop their strengths. Rather than creating stark categories of 'winners and losers', structures for assessment should be a launchpad, a means of highlighting present achievement as the foundation for a confident and lifelong commitment to continuing education and training.

Motivation is clearly an important base for directing improvements in schooling but we should be wary of detaching the problems of pupils' commitment to learning from their social setting – as Frank Coffield (Director of the new ESRC Initiative on *The Learning Society*) (1995) recently warned:

> There are...long-standing structural barriers and inequalities which prevent people learning which are embedded in British society...the class structure, inadequate funding, the institutionalised split between the academic and the vocational, and the systematic problems created for education by the labour market.

He went on to remind us that concentrating on what motivates young people is not enough:

> Concentrating on the motivation of pupils provides an over-simplified image; we need to add institutional expectations, and the notions of hierarchy, power and participation, which are all part of the hidden curriculum. Better still to view personal qualities and social structure as interacting elements in the single process of learning, which Jerome Bruner describes as 'a communal activity, a sharing of the culture'.

The question of power and relationships in the school and classroom needs to be on the agenda for school improvement. Many pupils spoke positively of the changes in their relationships with teachers during year 11; they felt themselves to be more in a 'partnership' – engaged in a joint venture to a common end. To extend this relationship to the earlier years of secondary school could promote a better learning environment for all pupils. As Brian Smith (1989) reminds us, the pupil–teacher relationship has in fact changed relatively little over the years:

> At its worst, the relationship at secondary level is one...in which the teacher is the imparter of knowledge and the pupil is the sponge-like recipient. That must change to one in which there is real partnership in learning with the pupils actively involved, and the teacher much more like a resource and a catalyst. (p.9)

If the learner's perspective can be used as the cornerstone on which to begin building a new approach to schooling and a new sense of partnership in learning then, perhaps, many more pupils will leave school prepared 'for living an autonomous life in our society' (Stenhouse, op. cit.).

References

Ames, C. (1986) 'Effective motivation: the contribution of the learning environment', in R. S. Feldman (ed.) *The Social Psychology of Education: Current Research and Theory*. Cambridge: Cambridge University Press.

Coffield, F. (1995) 'One vision beyond the barriers'. *Times Educational Supplement*, 3 March.

Hargreaves, D. H. (1982) *The Challenge for the Comprehensive School*. London: Routledge and Kegan Paul.

Nash, I. (1995) 'Quarter of FE pupils "miss classes"'. *Times Educational Supplement*, 12 May.

OFSTED (1995) *Access amd Achievement in Urban Education: Nature of Improvement*. Papers and report of the conference held 2–3 November, 1994. London: HMSO.

Smith, B. (1989) 'Preparing to leave school in the 1990s'. *Pastoral Care*, June, 6–12.

Stenhouse, L. A. (1975) *An Introduction to Curriculum Research and Development*. London: Heinemann Educational.

Conclusion

CHAPTER 13

Reviewing the conditions of learning in school

Jean Rudduck, Roland Chaplain and Gwen Wallace

It is tempting and comfortable for us to assume that being a teenager is much the same as it has always been, using recollections of our own adolescence to interpret the actions and attitudes of teenagers today, but in doing so we ignore the impact of the deep changes which have taken place in our society. An article written by Angela Neustatter in 1995 brought out the sharp contrasts between the pictures of childhood that would be recognised by a thirty-five year old and by a teenager in the 1990s. The children quoted in her article vividly express their awareness, maturity and perception as they cope with the pressures of growing up in this decade. The culture of childhood and adolescence has been re-defined (and not for the first time in social history) through the conditions of unemployment, single parenting, family breakdown and poverty. We need to try to understand where young people are coming from and how such understanding can help us with the task of school improvement.

Dilemmas about the status and responsibility of young people seem to be intensifying in the wake of the present government's endorsement of market cultures and consumers' rights. Where children are concerned, one of the problems is knowing who represents the consumer and whose voice should be heard in debates about policy or in contributing to critiques of policy-in-practice. Children in schools are not commonly regarded as 'socially competent' (see Freeman, 1988) when it comes to making decisions on a range of issues that affect their institutional lives; parents or primary carers, therefore, take on the role of 'consumer' by proxy. This traditional exclusion of young people from the consultative processes, this bracketing out of their voice, is founded upon an outdated view of childhood which fails to acknowledge children's capacity to reflect on issues affecting their lives.

In society generally – and this is mirrored in schools – there seem to be three dimensions that are in tension: the need for a clear and acceptable social order; the need for improved performance; and a commitment to rights and responsibilities that reflect young people's social, intellectual and physical maturity. As we said in the opening chapter, it is our view that the conditions of learning that prevail in the majority of secondary schools do not adequately take account of the maturity of young people, nor of the tensions and pressures that they experience as they struggle to reconcile the demands of their social and personal development with the development of their identities as learners. Out of school, so our data suggest, many young people find themselves involved in complex relationships and situations, whether within the family or the peer group. They carry quite tough responsibilities, balancing multiple roles and often finding themselves dealing with conflicting loyalties. In the texts of film, music and youth magazines there is an increasing readiness to take up and explore, in an open manner and language, many of the tensions of the adolescent world. In contrast, the structures of secondary schooling offer, on the whole, less responsibility and autonomy than many young people are accustomed to in their lives outside school, and less opportunity for learning-related tensions to be opened up and explored.

The chapters in this book have tried to look at some of the ways in which young people engage with the familiar and relatively unchanged organisational structures, routines and relationships of schooling. In general, they reflect the need for practitioners and policy-makers to recover taken-for-granted perceptions and practices from the realm of unreflected-on habit and to look critically at the values and assumptions embedded in social structures and institutional contexts. While most young people want to do well and are appreciative of the efforts of most teachers to help them, there is a need to review patterns of motivation and engagement in secondary schools and the broader institutional frameworks or regimes – what we call 'the conditions of learning' – that shape them. By this we mean the set of structures and relationships, common across the vast majority of secondary schools, that define what 'a pupil' is, that determine the regularities of learning, and that, crucially, exert a powerful influence on young people's sense of purpose in learning and their pattern of achievement.

The conditions of learning

Our data suggest that there are six principles which make a significant difference to learning. These are not novel and are likely to feature in most schools' statements of aims. What we have done is to come at them from the pupils' perspective and to reassert their central importance within a 'conditions of learning' frame – and to demonstrate the way that they interact with and strengthen each other. The principles are these:

1. **respect** for pupils as individuals and as a body occupying a significant position in the institution of the school;
2. **fairness** to all pupils irrespective of their class, gender, ethnicity or academic status;
3. **autonomy** – not as an absolute state but as both a right and a responsibility in relation to physical and social maturity;
4. **intellectual challenge** that helps pupils to experience learning as a dynamic, engaging and empowering activity;
5. **social support** in relation to both academic and emotional concerns;
6. **security** in relation to both the physical setting of the school and in interpersonal encounters (including anxiety about threats to pupils' self-esteem).

These principles operate within and through organisational structures and relationships and, according to the degree that they are present for each pupil, they serve to construct different patterns of commitment and confidence among young learners. We can present this diagrammatically, as in Figure 1; it is this set of relationships that constitutes what we call 'the conditions of learning'.

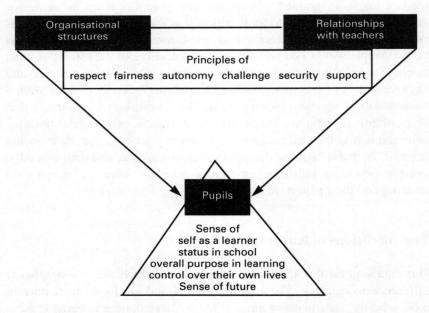

Figure 1 Framework for understanding 'the conditions of learning'

The list below identifies the aspects of **organisational structures** that most obviously shape the different patterns of opportunity and advantage that individual pupils experience in school and that affect their sense of self as a learner, sense of status within the institution and sense of purpose in learning. We are concerned about how:

- material and human resources are allocated to different groups of pupils and tasks and what priorities are reflected;
- different cohorts of pupils are divided and labelled;
- the system for informing pupils about and explaining the rationale for particular rules, regimes or new procedures operates (including homework, coursework, examinations and so on);
- time in school is organised for purposes of learning, organisation/administration and social activity; also the extent to which, for some groups of pupils, possible 'time on task' is reduced, and the way that time for learning is divided into a particular number of lessons of a particular length during each day and week;
- rewards and sanctions are handled and expectations of achievement are communicated.

By **relationships with teachers** we mean the interactions within school of teacher and pupil or teacher and pupils (we are not here focusing on pupil–pupil interactions). Our interviews suggest that what we should be concerned about are the *messages* that such interactions communicate to pupils about themselves, both as learners and as people. Certain kinds of interactions are highlighted in the interviews as carrying strong negative or positive tones – for instance:

- teachers being available to talk with pupils about learning and schoolwork, not just about behaviour;
- teachers recognising pupils' readiness to take more responsibility as they grow older and engage with them in as adult a way as possible;
- teachers being sensitive to the tone and manner of their discourse with pupils, as individuals and in groups, so that they do not humiliate them, criticise them in ways that make them feel small (especially in front of their peers), or shout at them;
- teachers being seen to be fair in all their dealings with all pupils (in particular, bearing in mind issues of gender, ethnicity and social class) and realising that one important aspect of fairness is not prejudging pupils on the basis of past incidents (i.e. pupils need to know that if they want to change their image and behaviours they are not constrained by teachers' expectations based on previous conduct);
- teachers ensuring that they make *all* pupils feel confident that they can do well and can achieve something worthwhile.

We have started each point with the word 'teachers'; this may seem one-sided but we have, earlier, discussed pupils' 'promises' that, if teachers treated them more openly and fairly and with more respect, then they would be more ready to respond constructively in school.

Finally, we turn to the quality of teaching. Although this is a highly significant element in the conditions of learning, we are aware that our data add little to what teachers and other researchers (see Cooper and McIntyre, 1993, for instance) already know and we consequently give little space to it in this discussion. We choose to emphasise just four features that we think are important enough to pupils to be worth restating – and that reflect the importance of the principles of respect and challenge. These are:

1. lessons that are well-prepared and are seen to be well-prepared, so that pupils know they have learned something and see that their teachers have put effort into preparing the lesson for them;

2. lessons that have a clear focus and a content that finds some way of engaging with pupils' everyday experiences;

3. lessons that have some variety of pace and activity (including opportunities for practical and/or interactive work); it may be useful to think of lessons as needing a strong sense of 'form' (an important but elusive word which suggests an appropriate matching of content, style and sequencing); they need to be well-structured, without waste of time but with passages of intense focus balanced by well-controlled and clearly signalled moments of respite;

4. the importance of teaching that signals to pupils that the teacher enjoys teaching the subject and enjoys teaching them.

Giving pupils a voice in school improvement

Adapting some lines from Auden, we could say that, traditionally, the voice of the pupil 'makes nothing happen: it survives / In the valley of its saying where executives / Would never want to tamper'. In arguing that what pupils say about schooling can be used as a basis for school improvement we are challenging that tradition.

As we have seen, what pupils say about teaching, learning and schooling is not shatteringly novel. Although familiar and full of a commonsense power of persuasion, it has attracted little serious attention from 'executives' at the level of either state or school. Such neglect merely confirms the low status of pupil opinion. But it may also be that we needed a context in which it seemed legitimate for pupil opinion to be taken into account: the 'school improvement' movement provides such a context. In saying this we are not trying to displace the more teacher-oriented and management-oriented analyses and guidance offered in chapter 1 which have become the key texts of school improvement; we are merely offering additional starting points.

In writing this final chapter we were aware of moving from the vivid detail of pupils' words and experiences to some rather vague and virtuous exhortations. And yet we wanted to draw pupils' observations together and put them into some kind of frame that allows us to see where, within the structures and relationships of schooling, action might be taken that could strengthen young people's sense of themselves as confident learners and strengthen their commitment to achieve. This meant going beyond their words to suggestions that seem to us to be the logical outcomes of what they have said in interview. And, as Shotter warned, we know that however much we – the teachers, the researchers – are committed to struggling for the empowerment of young people, and however much we convince ourselves that we are presenting their authentic voice, we are likely to be refracting their meanings through the lens of our own interests and concerns. It is easy to overlook the significance in pupils' accounts of schooling of what may seem to us relatively small concerns, mere fragments of routine experience. In the interviews pupils had no need to explain – why should they? – 'how and why these "trivial" things matter so much', nor to show how 'these small things work to influence them in their feelings as to "who" they are...' (Shotter, 1993, pxii).

While the data that we have drawn on in these chapters were gathered by researchers we think that, if the conditions in schools allow it, pupils 'could just as easily share their world with their teachers' – but with the proviso that teachers must perceive 'the pupils' world as worth becoming engaged with' (Sleeter and Grant, 1991, p. 67). Another proviso would be that the voices of *all* pupils should be listened to and not just those who are more academically and socially confident, for it is the less effective learners who are most likely to be able to explore aspects of the system that constrain commitment and progress; these are the voices least likely to be heard and yet most important to be heard.

In conclusion, we would claim that pupils (and we are generalising from those we interviewed) are urging us to review some of the assumptions and expectations that serve to hold habitual ways of thinking in place. The history of reform in education (in this country and in others – see Rudduck, 1991, pp. 21–35) is of change efforts that are only partially successful because they fail to grapple with the deep structures of schooling – assumptions about what a pupil is, for instance. We would argue that one of the weaknesses of reform efforts – and we have had our fair share of them – is that they have persistently neglected an important dimension of the situation. If we are to be confident that the vast majority of young people will commit themselves to learning while they are in the period of compulsory schooling and that they will take that commitment on when they leave school, then we have to take seriously young people's accounts and evaluations of teaching, learning and schooling. As Zephaniah said, in the lines quoted in the frontispiece:

> Teachers, your students have so much to say...
> If you are so concerned about their future
> Read about their concerns.

References

Auden, W. H. (1939; collected in 1958 edition) 'In memory of W. B. Yeats', in *W. H. Auden (a selection by the author)*, p. 67. Harmondsworth: Penguin.

Cooper, P. and McIntyre, D. (1993) 'Commonality in teachers' and pupils' perceptions of effective classroom learning'. *British Journal of Educational Psychology*, **63**, 381–399.

Freeman, A. (1988) 'Who's moving the goalposts and what game are we playing anyway?', in L.Barton, *The Politics of Special Educational Needs*. Lewes: Falmer Press.

Neustatter, A. (1995) 'Thanks for the Memories'. *The Independent*. (14th June) Section 2, pp. 2–3

Rudduck, J. (1991) *Innovation and Change*. Lewes: Falmer Press.

Shotter, J. (1993) *Cultural Politics of Everyday Life*. Buckingham: Open University Press.

Sleeter, C. E. and Grant, C. A. (1991) 'Mapping terrains of power: student cultural knowledge versus classroom knowledge', in C. E. Sleeter (ed.) *Empowerment through Multicultural Education*. Albany: State University of New York Press.

Zephaniah, B (1994) Opening lines in *Haggerston Voices*, a collection of poems written by Haggerston pupils during 1994 when Benjamin Zephaniah and Dimela Yekwai were visiting poets.

Name Index

Subject Index